The Burden of Memory, the Muse of Forgiveness

W.E.B. Du Bois Institute

Henry Louis Gates, Jr.
Series Editor

The Open Sore of A Continent
A Personal Narrative of the Nigerian Crisis
Wole Soyinka

From Emerson to King
Democracy, Race, and the Politics of Protest
Anita Haya Patterson

Primitivist Modernism
Black Culture and the Origin of Transatlantic Modernism
Sieglinde Lemke

The Burden
of Memory,
the Muse
of Forgiveness

Wole Soyinka

New York Oxford
Oxford University Press
1999

Oxford University Press

Oxford   New York
Athens   Auckland   Bangkok   Bogotá   Buenos Aires   Calcutta
Cape Town   Chennai   Dar es Salaam   Delhi   Florence   HongKong   Istanbul
Karachi   Kuala Lumpur   Madrid   Melbourne   Mexico City   Mumbai
Nairobi   Paris   São Paulo   Singapore   Taipei   Tokyo   Toronto   Warsaw

and associated companies in
Berlin   Ibadan

Copyright © 1999 by Wole Soyinka

Published by Oxford University Press, Inc.

198 Madison Avenue, New York, New York 10016

Oxford is a registered trademark of Oxford University Press

Library of Congress Cataloging-in-Publication Data
Soyinka, Wole.
The burden of memory, the muse of forgiveness/Wole Soyinka
p.   cm.—(W.E.B. Du Bois Institute)
Includes index.
ISBN 0-19-512205-4
1. Africa—Politics and government—1960- 2. Nigeria—Politics and govern-
ment—1984- 3. Reconciliation. 4. Amnesty—Africa. 5. African literature—
20th century—History and criticism. 6. Black literature—20th century—
History and criticism. 7. Politics and literature—Africa—History—20th cen-
tury. 8. Senghor, Léopold Sédar, 1906- . 9. Blacks in literature. I. Title. II.
Series: W.E.B. Du Bois Institute (Series)
DT30.5.S697 1998
960.3'2—dc21 97-50052

9 8 7 6 5 4 3 2 1

Printed in the United States of America
on acid-free paper

Contents

Foreword

The lectures in this collection were delivered as the inaugural for the Dubois Institute Macmillan lecture series at Harvard University in April 1997. A mere one year later, the list of personalities summoned to "testify" at this rhetorical Tribunal on Truth and Restitution begins to read like a memorial roll call—Mobutu Sese Seko, Pol Pot, Sanni Abacha, and so on, but most dramatic, and the one truly tragic death of all, Chief Moshood Kasimawo Abiola, the 1993 president-elect of the Nigerian nation.

I have decided to leave the lectures as delivered—that is, to keep such references in the "active sense" in which they were made. Apart

from underlining the vivid currency of the events
evoked in these talks as patterns of inhuman conduct that continue to scar and traumatize individuals and nations in an ever-escalating magnitude
of horrors, it serves (dare one hope?) as an unin-
tentional reminder to surviving emulators of the
chastening reckoning with mortality that awaits
both the sinned and the sinned against.

The scales of reckoning with mortality are
never evenly weighted, alas, and thus it is on the
shoulders of the living that the burden of justice
must continue to rest. Sacrifices to the cause of
equity, like Moshood Abiola, or the writer Ken
Saro-Wiwa and his eight companions, remind us
of the continuum of baffling exactions that are
wrung from the parties of the wronged, an unfinished business that raises a clamor of responsibility for redress against the peace of survivors.

The world my be forgiven for exuding a
sense of euphoria when prison gates, which once
appeared to enclose the entirety of a nation, give
the appearance of being suddenly flung open, but
the task remains for us to ensure that they are
never again slammed shut! Let us hope therefore
that peoples and nations that are yet weighed

down by the memories of a recent past understand this. Perhaps the debate that is intended in
the following pages may lead to the evolution of
mechanisms for the accompanying mission of
healing, of reconciling, but also of restitution.

Acknowledgments

When the author is a long-standing friend and colleague, revisiting a book on any shared interest or subject is just like taking up an old argument across a coffee table. It is therefore a double pleasure to acknowledge my indebtedness to Lilyan Kesteloot, whose seminal work *African Writers in the French Language* proved most useful in the preparation of these lectures and provided references I had long forgotten. Nearly all the discussants I know on the subject of *Negritude*—including its formulators—have undergone some form of conversion (from vestigial to total) from formerly held positions—laudatory or critical. Lilyan Kesteloot is no exception, and I know that she has herself revised some of the analysis laid out in that, her first book on the subject. The views expressed in this collection are therefore mine entirely, as well as the uses to which I have put her comments. Even where there are convergences, it is necessary to state that Ms. Kesteloot cannot thereby be held accountable for their present affirmation.

W.S.

The Burden of Memory, the Muse of Forgiveness

Introduction

In the 1992 presidential elections, it would
appear that the United States stood a reasonable
chance of acquiring a new president in the person
of a certain Mr. David Duke. Who knows, it may
yet happen. No, perhaps we should consider it
unlikely; but the state of Louisiana may eventually settle on him as its governor or reward his
industry with a senatorial seat—Mr. Duke appears
quite determined to move into the power structure at some level or another. For the moment,
however, he may be said to have declined into a
state of well-earned obscurity in the United
States. Not elsewhere though; not in Germany
where, a few years ago, it was reported that he

had made his presence felt in familiar ideological territory. Even more recently, Mr. Duke appears to have sought a new lease on life in South Africa.

What is remarkable about Mr. Duke and his bid to represent the Republican party as a presidential candidate? Simply that many Americans were startled to learn that he was a prominent and still active member of the Ku Klux Klan. He lost at the primaries of course, but his loss in the governorship race was a narrow one, and that fact remains a frightening reminder of the yet unconcluded business of racism, not only in the United States, but in much of Europe and the recently desegregated society of apartheid South Africa. After Mr. Duke's political setbacks in his own country, he cavorted briefly with the neo-Nazis and skinheads in Germany but found that the Germans, eager to renounce and distance themselves from any glorification of their shameful past, wisely kept him—in the main—at arm's length.

His invasion of South Africa has been very different. It is Mr. Duke's confident plunge—and we cite him only as an illustrative case—into that yet simmering cauldron of racism that presents us here with some uncomfortable ramifications of

South Africa's ongoing strategies for the reconciliation of that society and, by extension, the reconciliation of races.

Was the mission of Mr. Duke in South Africa by any chance to promote the cause of South Africa's Truth and Reconciliation Commission? No. Very much the contrary. Duke was visiting that country to express solidarity with a self-declared independent Free Boer Republic—inspired perhaps by the American Freemen enclave?—which had resolved that apartheid may be officially outlawed in the new South Africa but its extreme right-wing members, densely located in a town royally named Balmoral, had different ideas of what the relationship between races should be. A trace has revealed that some of these defenders of the white American way of life, the so called Freemen movement, are none other than offshoots of the Ku Klux Klan who have merely exchanged the ludicrous (but once lethal!) duncehead garb of the KKK for the macho camouflage from military surplus stores.

We do not know yet for certain, but it is not taking undue liberty with probability to suggest that Mr. Duke would hardly depart from South Africa without establishing a few branches of the

Ku Klux Klan. Even if he does not, his presence at this time will undoubtedly inspire the creation of chapters modeled, with a few Boer-culture variations, on the midnight riders of the Deep South *ancien regime*. In any case, boosting his mission, and such mimic tendencies, was an independent donation of several million dollars, the gift of an obscure but compassionate Southern lady to the white enclave to enable it to sustain its existence of defiance of black majority rule and the defense of a white supremacist culture now menaced, in the imagination of its proponents, by the barbaric hordes of a liberated race.

Now, the country of which Mr. Duke is a citizen—and *president manqué*—has a discriminatory list of human types to which it would not grant entry through its borders—such a list once included communists (also apartheid South Africa's bogey). Today, the list includes drug traffickers, hard-core criminals, and terrorists. Would one exaggerate by claiming that the Klu Klux Klan can be classified as a terrorist organization? Mr. Duke preaches a less virulent form of Klanism, we are informed, but the difference is one of those subtle shades that must be considered lost on actual victims of racism anywhere.

The U.S. media, as well as the government, were also in an uproar over a million-dollar donation made to Minister Farrakhan's movement by the Libyan government—there was no way he was going to be permitted to bring that terrorist money into the United States! Yet here was a U.S. citizen pouring her millions into a cause that must be considered treasonable—or at the least subversive—in a foreign, sovereign state. To the best of our information, the South African government has not raised a squeak. Surely, the United States, by any yardstick, must be considered a far less fragile society than South Africa. Its democracy has been tested and proved durable. Which of these two nations, shall we say, is pursuing a rational policy? How far can a nation stretch a policy of accommodation? Of these two nations, which, in short, has a greater justification for policies and actions that may be dictated by a touch of paranoia?

These questions have become pertinent in view of South Africa's mainly laudable project of reaching out toward even the proven deniers and enemies of a common humanity. If the new nation had chosen to adopt a different policy toward the past, one that is diametrically opposed to the *spirit* of Truth and Reconciliation, is it conceivable that Mr. Duke would have dared to even think of visting South Africa on a business mission, much less on one that makes no disguise whatsoever of traveling on the bandwagon of the gospel of hate? The contingent dramas of Truth and Reconciliation will mostly be played out, alas, outside the confines of the actual chambers where these hearings are held and beyond their actual duration. They will not always be as blatant as Mr. Duke's foray but, by often imperceptible motions, they will owe their eruption to spores of the same plant of a national forbearance that offers as much potential for social good and healing as it does for abuse and the enthronement of a cult of impunity. For there will always be those who read in these proceedings only a justification of any crimes, however heinous, as long as they can claim alliegiance to some form of private or collective belief, exigencies of state, or race/sect solidarity.

There are many such implications for a policy— of which South Africa's Truth and Reconciliation Commission is an instrument—for which there appears to be no built-in mechanism for a mandatory reciprocity. Knowledge, or information, is, however, a social virtue that carries a potential for prevention or social alertness, and this may actually counterbalance the risks inherent in a project that appears to dispense with the principle of restitution in historic accounting. But is knowledge on its own of lasting effect? Or is it simply that memory is short? Events in today's Nigeria, the escalating confidence of state terrorism, and wholesale erosion of human rights, ought, surely, to recall the trajectories of prior monstrosities on a continent's power landscape, their capacity for unthinkable atrocities. The unsavory ends of such rulers should serve as a lesson for their emulators, but somehow they never do. Anyone would think that Macias Nguema of Equitorial Guinea never existed, the voodoo tyrant who came to a grisly demise at the end of a rope. Then there was Master-Sergeant Doe over whom I proved a poor prophet because I had actually predicted for him the fate that finally overtook Macias Nguema *(The Apotheosis of Master-Sergeant Doe)*; he died a far more squalid death, butchered piecemeal by one faction of the would-be liberators of Liberia.

Emperor-for-Life Jean Bedel Bokassa was probably the most colorful of the lot, an imperial infanticide whose fate was surely a case of efficacious African *juju*—*à la* "Emperor Jones"—since he came back, of his own seeming volition, to the scene of his crimes and ended his days in one of the dingy cells into which, for personal diversion, he would lead his palace guards and trample alleged felons to death. His most notorious feat, however (apart from hammering a journalist into submission with a weighted end of a swagger stick at a public press conference), was his murder of schoolchildren. They had had the temerity to reject school uniforms for which he and his family held the sole franchise. As a good schoolmaster should, he rounded up the wayward pupils, locked them in prison for instruction, and, assisted by his goons, administered corporal punishment. That several died from this dose of imperial discipline merely vindicated the biblical injunction, "Spare the rod and spoil the child."

I dedicated a scene to that unimaginable atrocity in the play *Opera Wonyosi* but, try as one may, no fictionalized form can ever rival, as an instrument of public instruction, the format of a public tribunal of whatever shape and informed by whatever principle—be it of reconciliation or retribution. I recall a dinner discussion with a very good friend that almost ended in fisticuffs over the case of our greatest butcher of his time, Field Marshal Idi Amin Dada. Idi Amin, I had just remarked, was a practicing cannibal who actually kept the heads of his perceived enemies in his freezer for periodic contemplation. "Western propaganda!" my friend screamed. "How could you believe such preposterous fabrication?" In vain I tried to impress on him the reliability of my sources—which included children of African diplomats whom I had personally interviewed when I was editor of the magazine *Transition*. They were friends of Idi Amin's children with whom they sometimes exchanged visits—at least, until their parents' intervention. Nothing would shake the belief of my disputant that such a scourge of Western powers could not descend to such a level of barbarity—how else would the "Western press" be expected to take their revenge except by concoctions that showed African leaders as depraved beyond imagining?

The commission of inquiry that followed Idi Amin's departure has of course since revealed even more harrowing details of the last moments in the lives of Idi Amin's enemies and their resting places—if that expression may be thus misused. On that score alone, the necessity of such commissions is surely vindicated—to enthrone, once and for all, the desirable goal of Truth. Beyond Truth, the very process of its exposition becomes part of the necessity, and, depending on the nature of the past that it addresses, the impact it has made on the lives of the citizens and the toll it has taken on their sense of belonging, it may be regarded as being capable of guaranteeing or foundering the future of a nation. Indeed, it may be seen as a therapy against civic alienation. There is obviously a limit to the capabilities of even the most obsessed dramatist to transform public sensibilities toward the recognition of Truth, and, in any case, isn't the poor scribbler already tainted by his fictionalizing needs—select, distort, and exaggerate for effect? Not even the use of the actual stark, unvarnished dialogue (such as court proceedings) of a crime as in *The Death of Steve Biko* (Fenton and Blair) totally rescues the dramatist from suspicion of "making a case." The dramatist must still compress a hundred or more hours into two or three and thus must edit. Tribunals, even as printed documents, have the advantage of a *current* reality, and so—yes—this is a plea to African governments not to bury those documents in the musty archives of racial sensibilities. It is mandatory that we learn of the contents of Mobutu's Swiss vaults, but even more essential to national well-being and its capacity for transformation must be considered an exposition of the contents of Idi Amin's refrigerator! *The Truth shall set you free?* Maybe. But first the Truth must be set free.

Truth as prelude to reconciliation, that seems logical enough; but Truth as the justification, as the sole exaction or condition for Reconciliation? That is what constitutes a stumbling block in the South African proceedings. Unlike Master-Sergeant Doe or Emperor Bokassa, Idi Amin appears to be living in cozy retirement in Saudi Arabia. But suppose Uganda were to launch its Truth and Reconciliation Commission over the Idi Amin and Obote era, would either, if still alive, be entitled to return, confess his crimes, and be restored to the bosom of Uganda society, cleansed of all obligations to atone? Most African traditional societies have established modalities that guarantee the restoration of harmony after serious infractions—see, for instance, the banishment of Okonkwo after involuntary homicide in Chinua Achebe's *Things Fall Apart*. And, if we may be somewhat whimsical, Emperor Bokassa's bizarre return to the Central African Republic, in full knowledge of what fate awaited him, argues strongly for some kind of supernatural intervention—the vengeful souls of the violated children dragging him back from the security of his French asylum? Certainly, a singularly atrocious act appeared to be denied closure until the perpetrator returned to expiate on the scene of the crime. Maybe, in the sphere of abominations, (African) nature does abhor a vacuum. Are we then perhaps moving too far ahead of our violators in adopting a structure of response that tasks us with a collective generosity of spirit, especially in the face of *ongoing* violations of body and spirit?

Perhaps these are questions that, ultimately, can never be satisfactorily resolved—the teleology of the individual social mind is often at war with the collective. And then—to argue for the equitable stricture of law—since we deplore the application of *retroactive* law, a law that today punishes acts that were committed when such acts did not constitute crimes, do we tend to sense a moral distortion in a proceeding that pursues the opposite—pardons a crime through retroactive dispensation—this being without prejudice to the place of mitigation. Chile and Argentina are countries caught in a dilemma that is a cross between the politically expedient and the morally compelling. It must be pointed out also that several of the crimes being paraded through the hearings in South Africa today actually flouted the law and operational directives as spelled out even in apartheid times—in short, it is not simply that a case for the Eichmann defense—*I was merely carrying out the orders of a superior*—is not sustainable, it is also that it often cannot even be evoked.

The South African example, one that takes the bull by the horns by enunciating a clear direction of intent, obviously makes for compelling study. Other commissions make no claims beyond setting out the facts, a procedure that, in the main, grants no immunity beforehand (or very rarely, as a version of "plea bargaining") and does not foreclose the many possible mechanisms of some form of restitution by the inculpated. The "revolutionary" tribunal does not come into this purlieu, being usually an instrument of "revolutionary justice" that obeys no laws but the law of the victors, with or without the approbation of the liberated populace. South Africa was, of course, never a candidate for the revolutionary formula, since it owed its transformation more to negotiations than the route of arms.

History teaches us to beware of the excitation of the liberated and the injustices that often accompany their righteous thirst for justice. I was present at the "first coming" of Ghana's Flight-Lieutenant Jerry Rawlings and could hardly believe my eyes and ears at the spectacles of mob justice that took place, often with the incitement and participation of uniformed soldiers. At other times, they merely kept implacable watch. In the main, they set up their own "instant justice" courts within their barracks or in the market-places, especially during their all-out war against profiteering and hoarding. Unforgettably disturbing were the processions of a baying student population in headlong messianic plunge into the abyss of unreason: *Kill! Kill! Blood! Blood! More blood! Let the blood flow! More! More!* Having witnessed, at first hand, the callous despoilation of a proud and productive nation by the top military brass and its civilian cronies, the deliberate erosion of civilian self-confidence in the ability to survive the present, much less direct its future, the moment of truth was one that I had eagerly awaited and, indeed, one toward which, from our

Transition outpost, we had been able to make some modest contribution. In the end, one was left to wonder, in hindsight at least, if the approach of a *Truth and Reconciliation*, albeit with some fundamental changes in the essentials—something closer to Truth and *Restitution*—would not have served the Ghanaian populace better. The apogee of that movement's mode of restitution was, controversially, the public execution of six military officers, four of them generals. For one at least, there was absolutely no *justice*, since truth was not a factor in his trial. His execution was murder, a fact that was attested to, on several occasions, by the leader of the insurrection turned revolution of sorts, who was helpless, it would appear, confronted by the tide of unreason. Typical of the Jacobin mood from the *civilian* sector—by no means unanimous, admittedly—was the following exhortation from an editorial in the Ghanaian *Catholic Standard* (July 29, 1979),* authored by a Roman Catholic priest:

> This revolution is not a wedding party...this is the time to literally baptize

* Cited in Barbara Okeke, *June 4: A Revolution Betrayed*, Ikenga, 1982.

17

the whole nation.... We do not love those executed less, but we love our country more.... Of course, the executions are not the only solution, but they certainly form part of the solution.

And from a medical doctor's contribution to *West Africa* (London, July 2, 1979):

I endorse absolutely the determination of the Armed revolutionary Council to wash the country clean with the blood of the corrupt.... I have been telling my friends for some time now that Ghana's only cleansing lotion is the blood of those who so badly let her down through selfishness and corruption.... Ghana is so heavily soiled that the blood of 500 can be enough only for the removal of surface dust. To remove the grime and ingrained dirt, the AFRC has to go a great deal further.

Enough, I think, of the obverse face of Truth and Reconciliation, always recollecting that the Ghanaian upheaval was a vastly different scenario from the South African. The only ground they share is that of recognition of a need for a purgation of the past, the creation of a new sense of being, but they do serve us as two extreme options for the initiation of such a process after the collapse of a discredited and criminal order. Would the Truth and Reconciliation ethic have been applicable, even thinkable in post-Acheampong Ghana? In post-Mobutu Zaire? Will it be adaptable in post-Abacha Nigeria? That circumstances may make such a proceeding expedient is not to be denied, but we must not shy away from some questions: would it be *just*? And, more important, how does it implicate both the present and the future?

The crimes that the African continent commits against her kind are of a dimension and, unfortunately, of a nature that appears to constantly provoke memories of the historic wrongs inflicted on that continent by others. There are moments when it almost appears as if there is a diabolical continuity (and inevitability?) to it all—that the conduct of latter-day (internal) slaverunners is merely the stubborn precipitate of a yet unexpiated past. The ancient slave stockades do not seem ever to have vanished; they appear more to have expanded, occupying indiscriminate spaces that often appear contingent with national boundaries. Thus, the role of memory, of ancient precedents of current criminality, obviously governs our responses to the immediate and often more savage assaults on our humanity, and to the strategies for remedial action. Faced with such a balancing imposition—the weight of memory against the violations of the present—it is sometimes useful to invoke the voices of the griots, the ancestral shades and their latter-day interpreters, the poets. Memory obviously rejects amnesia, but it remains amenable to closure that is, apparently, the ultimate goal of social strategies such as Truth and Reconciliation, and the Reparations Movement (for the enslavement of a continent). It is there that they find common ground even though the latter does entail, by contrast, a demand for restitution. Both seek the cathartic bliss, the healing that comes with closure.

The black poet—both within the continent and the diaspora—has been thrust into the heart of this hunger for closure, and has responded in a diversity of ways that testify to the poet's unique formation in colonialism and displacement (or alienation) and self-restoration through a human-

istic ethos that sometimes appears to be a deliberate act of fatih, more a quest than a cultural given.
How broadly, how generously that humanistic
cloak should be spread remains the grist of poetic
argument—poet versus poet—as each interprets a
common experience through the prisms of traditional thought as well as those of other distilla-
tions of knowledge, wisdom, and faith (including
ideology)—sometimes of the very violators of
that continent's own humanity. Unlike the the-
ologian, who takes his voice from the realms of
deities, the poet appropriates the voice of the people and the full burden of their memory. Where
he invokes the gods and the ancestors (as in the
case of René Depestre or Birago Diop), it is usually to make them serve the agenda of peoples, to
execute their judgment on history and minister to
the pangs of their memory. The strategy of a
poet-cum-theologian as, in a very special sense,
Léopold Sédar Senghor may be considered, therefore serves as a bridge for the impulse that sepa-
rates the memory-driven poet and the would-be
transcedentalist over history. *To err is human, to
atone, humane,* declares one: *to err is human, to
forgive, African,* responds the other. Is a

continent's humanity of such bottomless reserves that it can truly accommodate the latter? The poets have confronted, in advance of the event, the great humanistic dilemma of South Africa, and it would appear, in the main, that the poet sometimes anticipates or vindicates the vision of the statesman.

I

Reparations, Truth, and Reconciliation

From within the same continent, two strategies of confrontation with one's history. They are off-springs of the same age, sprung from minds of a shared identity, and they appear to complement yet contradict each other. Both depend on a process of baring the truth of one's history in order to exorcise the past and secure a collective peace of mind, the healing of a bruised racial psyche. Both concepts even appear to play a game with each other—in the mind at least—since some form of mental reconciliation appears to be provoked for their cohabitation. How on earth does one reconcile reparations, or recompense, with reconciliation or remission of wrongs? Dare we presume that both, in their differing ways, are committed to ensuring the righting of wrongs and the triumph of justice?

The undeniable differences merely complicate matters—one proposal originates from a history of Africa that has become somewhat remote, attenuated by time and becoming blurred by global relationships, while the other owes its birth to an ordeal that is so immediate that both victims and violators are alive and locked within the necessity of cohabitation. This contrast in itself provides a paradox—in expectations. If anything, it is the latter condition, the contemporary one, that should mandate a call for reparations in one form or another. The victims are alive and in need of rehabilitation while their violators—as a recognizable group—pursue a privileged existence, secure in the spoils of a sordid history. Indeed, it is within the enclosure of that nation called South Africa that the principle of reparations presents itself as something quite practical and feasible, indeed, clamorous, unlike the context of slavery that continues to be increasingly contumacious in the determination of responsibilities.

Just to let one's fantasy roam a little—what

really would be preposterous or ethically inadmissible in imposing a general levy on South Africa's white population? This is not intended as a concrete proposal, but as an exercise in pure speculation. We are, after all, engaged in identifying all possible routes to social harmonization—from the obvious to the unthinkable. A collective levy need not be regarded as a punitive measure; indeed— since the purpose is reconciliation, such an offer could originate from the beneficiaries of Apartheid themselves, in a voluntary gesture of atonement—it need not be a project of the state. Is such a genesis—from within the indicted group itself—truly beyond conception? If, however, this attribution of self-redeeming possibilities within the psychology of guilt remains within the utopian imagination, and some external prodding proved necessary, the initiative could be taken up by someone of the non-establishment stature of Archbishop Desmond Tutu. The respected cleric and mediator mounts his pulpit one day and addresses his compatriots on that very theme: "White brothers and sisters in the Lord, you have sinned, but we are willing to forgive. The scriptures warn us that the wages of sin are death but, in your case, they seems to be wealth. If therefore you chose to shed a little of that sinful wealth as a first step toward atonement... etc. etc."

We know that strategies for the transformation of society often demand a measure of pragmatism or, to put it crudely, deals. Secret, sometimes unrecorded, but deals nevertheless, a guarantee between the lines, legible only to signatories to the public document. Indemnity is often granted to the undeserving in order to minimize damage to the structure of society and even preserve lives—Argentina, Chile, these are all pertinent examples that nevertheless constitute an outrage to the moral sense and stress the limits of our humanity. Ideally, we wish that the Galtieris, the Pinochets of the world would encounter nothing less than the fate of the Nicolae Ceaucescus, the Sergeant Does, and other human pollutions of the planet. Despite that recognition, however, despite the realization that South Africa is, like any other zone of state-engendered anomie, unique in the intricacy of motions—both internal and external—that led to her liberation, there remains a sense that the adopted formula for the harmonization of that society erodes, in some way, one of the pillars on

which a durable society must be founded—
Responsibility. And ultimately—Justice.

A fact that is often conveniently ignored is
that the territory of culpability in the South
African instance was not limited to the state. One
of the most courageous admissions that I know
of in the aftermath of revolutionary struggles was
that of President Nelson Mandela, who openly
confronted the ANC with its own dismal record
of needless cruelty and abuse of human rights,
especially in prisons and detention camps run by
the movement within friendly front-line states
such as Zambia. Torture and arbitrary executions
were, apparently, commonplace, and it is not easy
to forget the untidily resolved murder of the
luckless "Stompie," beaten to death by members
of Winnie [Madikizela] Mandela's football
club—in reality, her bodyguards. The murder of
the white American volunteer girl, stabbed to
death by four Soweto thugs who were later
imprisoned for the crime, is an even more harrowing reminder. A recent televised appearance
of the four murderers at a meeting with the parents of the victim, exploiting in their turn the
rites of open confession with the prospect of an
amnesty, actually goes to the heart of a nation's

moral dilemma. The parents bestowed their forgiveness, and it does seem likely that, by classifying the crime as a "political" one, the perpetrators may also be deemed to have fulfilled all the conditions that qualify them for a remission of their sentence. Must the psychopathic opportunists of a revolutionary struggle also become beneficiaries of the balm of victory? A cowardly killing, surely, can be defined even by the internal moralities of any liberation struggle, however violent, otherwise, let us, at once and for all time, abandon all concepts of, and the exceptional deeds that attach to, heroism!

Let us, for a brief moment, superimpose the face of Pol Pot over any one of these public applicants for remission in a parallel process in Cambodia. Is it really given to the human mind to accommodate, much less annul, such a magnitude of man-inflicted anguish? The logic of "Truth and Reconciliation," however, demands that the mind prepare itself for the spectacle of a "penitent" Pol Pot, freed, morally cleansed, at liberty to go about his business in a humanely restored milieu!

This risk-free parade of villains, calmly—and occasionally with ill-concealed relish—recounting their roles in kidnappings, tortures, murders, and mutilation, at the end of which absolution is granted without penalty or forfeit, is either a lesson in human ennoblement, or a glorification of impunity. Admittedly, it does constitute at the very least, a revelation of the infinite possibilities of human options in the resolution of social crises—and this perhaps must remain our consolation. Even if judgment comes down eventually on the negative import of such a proceeding, there is still an inherent challenge in it that cannot be denied. It is not, after all, an occurrence in a historic vacuum. Within the borders of South Africa's northward neighbor, Malawi, the once President-for-Life Hastings Banda did go on trial for his life: he was acquitted, yes—largely on a technicality—but the process of reducing the once all-powerful controller of freedom and restraint, of life and death to an egalitarian uncertainty with his erstwhile victims, is a model of social restitution whose validity cannot be contested. Never was that ubiquitous rubric on West African passenger vehicles—*No Condition Is Permanent*—more robustly vindicated!

The Ethiopian model is also chillingly

instructive. The trial of Mariam Mengistu—*in absentia*—obviously lacks the therapeutic symmetry that his physical presence would have provided, but the criminal dock is occupied by several of his principal associates in mass murder. The testimonies from Ethiopia open a unique chapter in state criminality, at least on the African continent. Never was mass murder more meticulously bureaucratized; the records reveal a rare punctiliousness of executive psychopathy—a total contrast with the arbitrariness of the Idi Amin regime, for example, or the Mobutu. The hour, the methods of dispatch, the disposition of the victims, and the disposal of their remains are recorded, the details of torture as well as measures of reprisals against colleagues or relations who dared exhibit signs of sympathy or grieving. We do accept that even the dismal recital or publication of these records would bring a measure of consolation that attaches to the recognition of past suffering, but this could never substitute for, nor indeed induce, the sense of closure, the catharsis that only the presence of the inculpated, now pressed into service in a reversal of roles, would provide. It goes beyond mere rites of vengeance; it is a process of vindication—vindication of the prolonged agony (and implicit resistant will) of society, whose end-product is restoration of its violated integrity.

And there are other models—like Rwanda, in which the international community has again recognized and pursued a role in a process that establishes that there are certain crimes that have ramifications beyond the borders of any nation and constitute crimes against humanity. The problem with the South African choice is therefore its implicit, *a priori* exclusion of criminality and, thus, responsibility. Justice assigns responsibility, and few will deny that justice is an essential ingredient of social cohesion—indeed, I have asserted elsewhere that justice constitutes "the first condition of humanity." And even as justice is not served by punishing the accused before the establishment of guilt, neither is it served by discharging the guilty without evidence of mitigation—or remorse.

We recognize that the application of what, in effect, is an attribution of mitigation before the proof has, in this case, only one end in view, and that is to encourage revelation, to establish truth.

Could it be then that, underlying it all, is the working out of that christian* theological precept: "The Truth shall make you free"? Or do we seek answers, for this unusual lesson of our time, in a humanism that our own poets and philosophers have ascribed, in moments of race euphoria or contestation with the European world, as being uniquely African? Poets and statesmen of the temperament of Léopold Sédar Senghor would, I am certain, endorse this largeness of black generosity. If the government of Nelson Mandela sought vindication among Africa's poets for its "Truth and Reconciliation" option, Senghor's poetry would provide it more than amply; advocating, as it does, a philosophy of wholesale remission. And Senghor would root this, undoubtedly, within that generous earth of Africa's humanity that he regards as an enduring critique of Europe's soullessness. Well, the Africa of Senghor's Muse is hardly recognizable in the realities that surround us today, and with Rwanda hardly a memory beat away from even the most uninformed, we would

---

* The convention that capitalizes this and other so-called world religions is justified only when the same principle is applied to other religions, among them, the Orisa.

be wise to tread warily along that path, or at least
call to our aid the corrective views of contemporary witnesses—also black—such as Keith
Richburg!*

But will the South African doctrine work,
ultimately? Will society be truly purified as a result
of this open articulation of what is known? For
even while we speak of "revelation," it is only revelation in concrete particulars, the ascription of
faces to deeds, admission by individual personae
of roles within known criminalities, affirmation by
the already identified of what they had formerly
denied. Nothing, in reality, is new. The difference
is that knowledge is being shared, collectively, and
entered formally into the archives of that nation.
So, back to the question, this procedural articulation of the known, will it truly heal society? Will
it achieve the reconciliation that is the goal of the
initiators of this heroic process? For it is heroic—
let that value be frankly attributed. Even those of
us who, conceding our unsaintliness, distance
ourselves from the christian—or indeed bud-
dhist—beatitudes, do acknowledge that forgiveness is a value that is far more humanly exacting

* Keith Richburg, *Out of America* (Basic Books, 1997).

than vengeance. And so—will this undertaking truly "reconcile" the warring tribes of that community? My inclination is very much toward a negative prognosis. An ingredient is missing in this crucible of harmonization and that ingredient is both material and moral.

The moral element is glaring enough, though it is much too nebulous to assess—that element being remorse and, thus, repentance. Nebulous because one can only observe that an expression of remorse has been made. Is it genuine? Impossible to tell. I have not been at any of the Truth and Reconciliation hearings but have followed reports—and by eyewitnesses. Indeed, the Nigerian opposition group to which I belong, with an eye already on the future of the nation after the expulsion of the current dictator* and his gang of torturers and assassins, decided from the start to closely monitor the proceedings, our hope being to extract some lessons that may prove useful under the political dispensation toward which our own nation is currently embattled. The cata-

* General Sanni Abacha, since deceased (June 8, 1998), allegedly of a heart attack. From Maiduguri (in the north) to Lagos (in the south), there was dancing in the streets, including even the military barracks!

logue of crimes being committed against the Nigerian people during the current and preceding insanities of power has to be addressed at some future time—my attention to this theme is, obviously, not without a touch of political self-interest. And the reports that emerge—from observers of all races and divergent political tendencies—is that there is very little evidence of remorse at these public confessionals. Hardly any sense of credible transformation revealed among the actors in this unprecedented drama. Admittedly, these will always remain subjective impressions, but if the televised coverage I have watched, which included interviews with the self-confessed criminals, can be accepted as reliable evidence, I remain convinced that the answer to the missing question—at least one that I never heard put—would be, "Oh yes, given the same circumstances, I would do the same thing all over again." However, let us abandon the hazy zone of remorse for now, and move to the material.

And here, I believe, is where the cry for Reparations for a different and more ancient cause suggests itself as the missing link between Truth and Reconciliation. The actual structuring of Reparations is secondary—in the case of South

Africa, it is not too difficult to identify targets—
from the collective to the individual—from state
agencies to businesses and voluntary associa-
tions—be they all-white political parties, segregat-
ed clubs and resorts, etc., self-defense militias (the
volunteer backbone of the state system)...a host of
privileged and/or profit-generating institutions
that prospered through Apartheid. The essential
is to establish the principle: that some measure of
restitution is always essential after dispossession.
Even the slave society of the United States of
America recognized this, although "forty acres
and a mule" is hardly what I would consider ade-
quate recompense for centuries of displacement,
dehumanization, and forced labor. The derisive
quality of manumission, its grudging tokenism,
would have its later consequences; it undoubtedly contributed to various dogged strategies of a
renewed race enslavement whose summation was
decidedly a denial of humanity. It encouraged Jim
Crowism, made possible the outrage of the
Tuskegee (syphilis) experimentation on unsus-
pecting blacks, whose sixty-year-long shame is
only now being partially exorcised by the admin-
istration of President Clinton. The tenacity of the
Ku Klux Klan, its tentacular hold over power

structures across the United States and its eventual threat to even the democratic complacency of government—until its virtual demise—remains a *caveat* against the dismissive option for a collective wrong. The culture of impunity in race relations remained firmly rooted in American society until the explosion of the sixties; by no stretch of the imagination can one suggest that it is, even today, near conclusively erased. Was an opportunity for internal reparations missed at a crucial moment? It is possible that today's calls for reparations from the African continent would have failed to resonate in America if the freeing of slaves had been accompanied by a different quality of integration into American society. In all likelihood, the children of the black Diaspora, from their state of infinite contentment, of total harmonization with a new social environment, would have told their kinfolk on the other side to shut up, reminding them that their ancestors shared responsibility for selling them off to European slavers, that any compensation, in any case, should be made strictly to the descendants of those who had endured the horrors of passage and the degradations of plantation. Nonetheless, all of the foregoing conceded, the continent itself is not without some sustainable claims in her own right, based on distortions in her organic development that are still traceable to the ravages of slavery.

It is not difficult to establish an abundance of reasons why the history of slavery must continue to plague the memory of the world. Principal among these is the simple fact that the history of humanity is incomplete without its acknowledgment, and the history of the African continent, including its economic history, would remain truncated. Next, objectively, the Atlantic slave trade remains an inescapable critique of European humanism. In a different context, I have railed against the thesis that it was the Jewish Holocaust that placed the first question mark on all claims of European humanism—from the Renaissance through the Enlightenment to present-day multicultural orientation. Insistence on that thesis, we must continue to maintain, merely provides further proof that the European mind has yet to come into full cognition of the African world as an equal sector of a universal humanity, for, if it had, its historic recollection would have placed the failure of European humanism centuries earlier—and that would be at the very inception of the

Atlantic slave trade. This, we remind ourselves, was an enterprise that voided a continent, it is estimated, of some twenty million souls and transported them across the Atlantic under conditions of brutality that have yet to be beggared by any other encounter between races. Reparations, then, as a structure of memory and critique, may be regarded as a necessity for the credibility of Eurocentric historicism, and a corrective for its exclusionist worldview.

More than quantifiable humanity was lost to that continent. The slave trade also imposed a rupture in the organic economic systems of much of the continent. It is a distortion that—partially at least, and compounded later by the imposition of colonial priorities in raw materials for Europe's industrial needs and the advent of multinational conglomerates—must surely account today for the intractable economic problems of that continent. Was the "partitioning of Africa" by the imperial powers simply a geographical violation of a people's right of coming-into-being as nations? Only if we insist on believing that the political instability within the so-called nations that make up the continent today owes nothing whatsoever to the artificiality, the sheer *illogic* of their boundaries! It is therefore appropriate to add partitioning to the wrongs that underly the cry for reparations from Africa, and surely such a claim would be unanswerable. My only problem with this is that African nations, since independence, have possessed it within their will to redress this particular wrong where evidently and bitterly contested, to launch their own internal reparations for the deprivation of organic identities and its costly consequences. Obviously no outsider, least of all the original perpetrators of this misdeed, can be entrusted with such an undertaking. Another Berlin conference of former colonizers to redraw the present boundaries of a continent? That would transgress even the generous boundaries of absurdity. Beginning with the Organization of African Unity, which formally consecrated this act of arrogant aggression, reinforced by civil wars on varied scales of mutual destruction in defense of the imperial mandate, the continent as a whole appears, however, to have swallowed intact this explosive seed of disunity— under the ironic banner of unity. If only African leaders could become acquainted with how much—just to illustrate the hollowness of such beginnings—the division of India and Pakistan (and the allocation of their respective boundaries) owed to the whimsical decisions of a mere civil servant imported straight from Whitehall, someone who had never even visited the Asian continent until then, but was selected for the "objective" distancing that that very ignorance was presumed to confer on him, was given a deadline of a mere twenty-eight days to complete his task in order to ensure that that continent was effectively divided before Independence Day—such leaders and cheerleaders would learn to be less cocky about the mangy claims of "national sovereignty." Much of the division of Africa owed more to a case of brandy and a box of cigars than to any intrinsic claims of what the boundaries enclosed. Or perhaps the same civil servant could be invited out of retirement and given absolute and binding powers to sort out the mess of African boundaries that enclose us today? The results would be no worse, I am certain, than the bequest of the imperial heads of 1889.

Cultural and spiritual violation—we may as well complete the catalogue—has left indelible imprints on the collective psyche and sense of identity of the peoples, a process that was ensured through savage repressions of cohering traditions by successive waves of colonizing hordes. Their *presence* was both physical and abstract. Their mission was not merely to implant their own peoples on any lands whose climates were congenial—East and Southern Africa—but to establish outposts for surrogate controls where the environment proved physically inclement. West Africa owed much to its humidity and the mosquito, a fact that was often celebrated by the early generational wave of nationalists. One political party in pre-independence Nigeria actually selected the mosquito for its party symbol. The British were not amused, and promptly proscribed it.

The cultural and spiritual savaging of the continent, let us hasten to insist, was not by the christian-European axis alone. The Arab-islamic dimension preceded it, and was every bit as devastating, a fact that a rather distorted sense of continental solidarity leads some scholars to edit, at the expense of Truth and reality. We must spend a little time recalling this revisionist trend, and silencing it. And for that exercise, we are obliged to begin by defining ourselves. The exercise is not new, but is constantly submerged under the allegedly superior claims of pan-Africanism

and anti-colonial rhetoric, the supposedly unify-
ing identity of victims of a common experience.
Yet even pan-Africanism demands that we first
resolve within ourselves the definition of "Africa"
that is at the heart of such constructs. We know
what is described as such on the atlas maps produced by the same mills owned by those who par-
titioned the continent. What remains yet unset-
tled (not that it is hidden) is just who are the peoples who define themselves, within that same continental boundary, variously as Africans, as being
also Africans or, as *something other than.*

Africa's Whereabouts

Just what, in short, is this Africa on behalf of
whom reparations have been demanded? Who
knows? In resolving just whom that Africa
embraces, we may approach an acceptable definition proffered by the singularity of a particular
experience of the victim race, shared by no one
else. Where does that Africa begin and how far
does it extend? Just how large and varied is this
family of victims? Even if we find it near impossible to decide to whom reparations should actually

be made, we can tackle the easier task, it being largely theoretical—identify on whose behalf reparations are being claimed. Is it for an entire continent? Is it for portions of it? Do we have, on that same continent—if indeed we decide that reparations are essential for the enthronement of a new, harmonized order of relationships—do we have on that same landmass called Africa those from whom reparations should also be demanded?

Not all African voices are united on, or comfortable with, these questions, but Truth goes with Reconciliation, and there can be no evasion. Those who preach the gospel of reparations must be prepared to accompany their claim to its logical conclusion. At a conference on that very subject held in Abuja, the capital of Nigeria, in—I believe—1991, an uncomfortable moment was reached when the issue of Arab participation in the slave trade could no longer be evaded. Let us pause and note here, by the way, that the movement for Reparations on the African continent was initiated, spearheaded, and heavily funded by that maverick of a businessman turned politician—an early pan-Africanist by the way, a fact about him that is little publicized—but more pertinently, the elected President of Nigeria, Chief

Moshood Abiola. At this moment,* he is spending his third year in the dungeons of the dictator, Sanni Abacha, for the crime of winning the 1993 presidential elections and insisting on his mandate. Abiola's campaign was taken up by the government of Nigeria at a meeting of the Organization of African Unity in Abuja in 1992 and, since then, the Reparations movement has become an intergovernmental project, with a commission in the OAU.

Now that provokes a number of ethical issues. There has to be a moral foundation to all quests for equity—he who comes to the court of equity, says the Latin proverb, must approach with clean hands. A crusade that is based on moral rights is obviously undermined by the impurity of conduct in its proponents—it is a theme that we must take up at the appropriate place.

To return to that conference, over which Moshood Abiola presided, the issue of Arab

---

* On the eve of his release from prison detention, one month after the death of his jailer Sanni Abacha, Moshood Abiola died suddenly, allegedly also of "cardiac arrest." The implications of his death for the nation will unfold into the next century, but the signs are clearly ominous.

45

participation in the slave trade was finally addressed. Sitting on the commission as a member of the International Committee on Reparations was a Tunisian diplomat, an Arab, and he found himself compelled to confront the paradox of his presence as a member of that committee. His response was a safe one, not original but safe. Unlike some African apologists and, indeed, a handful of African-American scholars and ideologues of a notorious persuasion, he did not attempt a pointless denial of a historic reality. He simply countered with a proposition that, since we are all victims of colonial oppression, we should act together in solidarity against the common oppressor, and obliterate that part of our divisive history. Of course, he then had to confront the logical follow-up—that the entire nature of the Reparations movement should be changed, that it should even be renamed altogether. Reparations Movement for Victims of Colonialism perhaps? But then this would dilute the original cause and require a totally different orientation and strategy, it would expand to embrace the indigenes of both North and South America, Australia, and New Zealand...in short, this was one way of ensuring that the manifesto for Reparations ended up as a permanent study document on the tables of the United Nations.

We are all Africans, so let's stick together and not indulge in the divisive issues of who enslaved whom—that is a proposition that one encounters quite frequently, and it is simply a case of special pleading that just as frequently evokes the justified and irreproachable response—*No, not all the peoples of Asia are Asians.* In resolving a definition of ourselves, that is, resolving the issue of identity of the reparations lineages—be it as victim, the censurable, or claimants of a special mitigation status—let us at least clear away some obscurantist categories, such as religion. I should make it clear, by the way, that the "who is African?" question is not an agonizing issue for me personally, having determined ages ago to answer African only when so addressed, and in a noncontroversial context. With that admission, I hope I may be considered capable of addressing the controversy with some dispassion. Does a first- or tenth-generation Moroccan or Algerian in the United States answer African-American? Does he celebrate *kwanza* or pursue soul food in preference to *meze* or *cous-cous?* These and allied parameters of cultural identity make fascinating considerations but are not matters of life and death.

The issue of religion is one, however, to which I confess a passionate partisanship, but only owing to an increasingly developed acuity of feeling over a continuing tradition of denial of, and disrespect toward a continent's own spirituality. Since the argument for remission or "exempt status" has also been taken through the religious route—adding insult to injury!—it is only just that we examine just how much such arguments are worth beyond the scholarly energy and the media time that project it. Just what is *African,* for a start, about any section of that continent that arrogantly considers any change of faith an apostasy, punishable even by death? What is *African* about religious intolerance and deadly fanaticism? The spirituality of the black continent, as attested, for instance, in the religion of the *orisa,* abhors such principles of coercion or exclusion, and recognizes all manifestations of spiritual urgings as attributes of the complex disposition of godhead. *Tolerance* is synonymous with the spirituality of the black continent, *intolerance* is anathema!

But, of course, this is never sufficient to silence those who can only read the *spirituality* of a continent and a people in the skyline of church steeples and the minarets of mosques. So let us proceed by way of analogy, using the United States, since, sometimes, the actualities of the African continent are simply too remote for many in these parts to grasp. Now, we often hear the United States referred to as a christian nation. What, however, does that religio-cultural parlance disguise within that very nation? The claim may be true, of course, given the fact that the majority of U.S. citizens are indeed christians—practicing or nominal. It is also a fact that this dominant religion is being given a good run for its money by yet another well-organized religion—islam—especially among the black, and the black prison population. Both religious facets of a contemporary reality, however, have bonded together to obscure one historical accusation—that the indigenous beliefs of the landmass known as the United States are neither christianity nor islam. Today, the original belief systems and worldviews of the autochthones exist, for the majority of inhabitants of the United States, as mere curios, relegated to anthropological studies within protected reservations, and treated just as marginally as the humanity that still observes them. Occasionally, the odd agency or institution admits as much and attempts a corrective—a recent instance being the peyote concession now made by the military establishment, one that enables its indigenous segment to commune (openly) with their godhead through the fumes of peyote. Even "political correctness" does land on its feet, occasionally and alas! Also, as the ecology becomes menaced, a few cranks here and there hold up these indigenes as examples of what should be the organic relationship between man and environment, rooted in indigenous culture and religion but, beyond that, what remains of that culture and worldview in the mainstream of American spirituality? Nothing. Certainly nothing that is acknowledged or affective in the overall culture of society—barring of course the cooption of the indigenous names of Indian tribes by football teams and car/plane manufacturers. Some cities, streets, hills, and rivers, it must be admitted, also bear the names of the ancestral inhabitants of the landmass but, for the average American, those names could just as easily belong to the valleys of storms and mountain peaks on the lunar landscape.

Conversely, however, from the point of view of the Sioux, the Apache, or the Cheyenne, both christianity and islam are alien religions on the land, and it does not surprise them in the least that their adherents interact with their environment in a way that is, at best, nature-indifferent or, at worst, nature-defiling. The Sioux, Apache, or Cheyenne suffer, however, from the disadvantage of having been turned into a minority on their own continent; Africans, praise the *orisa*, albeit in christian or moslem attires, have survived centuries of decimation by the slave raiders and their descendants, and continue to repopulate their land. Their spirituality is still expressed even within their modes of adaptation to, and of, those very religions that commenced their history of alienation.

This analogy should assist in clarifying why, to the indigenous sensibility of the autochthones of the African continent, the quest for exemption that comes by the religious route—that is, a plea by one or the other religion that its adherents brought a spiritual value to the continent that is more indigenous to the people than that imposed by its rival—is not only preposterous, it is blasphemous. Both religions came and subverted the organic systems of belief that pre-existed their arrival, religions older and, in many aspects, more humane than the manifested tenets of their own. The Euro-christian armies of conquest, fast on the heels of missionaries and early adventurers, plundered and looted ancient African civilizations, burnt and smashed priceless carvings, which, from their point of view, were nothing but manifestations of idolatory and satanism. Conversion to christiany was, admittedly, sometimes by persuasion, more often it was enforced—through military conquest, terror of enslavement, and punitive (economic) controls. A religion that separated humanity into the saved and the damned—the latter being qualified for mass deportation to distant lands as beasts of burden—can hardly be considered fundamentally compatible with the people on whom such a choice was imposed.

Was the Arab-islamic record an improvement? Georges Hardy's comment on its iconoclastic rampage sums up that record impartially: "Islam began the work of destruction. But

Europe did a better job."* The fate that overtook the arts was the same as that inflicted on society overall. From the west coast of Africa to southern Africa, the story is the same. Conversions for the glory of an equally alien deity. Nothing that the islamic invaders encountered was sacred; all was profane except the sword and the book of Allah. They set the precedent for compelling convertites to shed their indigenous names, names that narrated their beginnings and conferred on them their individual and historic identities. They inaugurated the era of slave raids on the black continent for Arab slave markets. The routes of slave caravans began from the central and eastern heartlands of the continent, stretched through Northern Africa to Saudi Arabia, or passed over the waters by slave dhows from Madagascar and Dar es Salaam to Yemen, Omar, etc. Even today, you will encounter ghettoes in many Arab countries peopled entirely by descendants of those slaves.

There is clearly no case here for the granting

* Georges Hardy, *L'Art nègre* (Paris: Editions H. Laurens, 1927).

of remission through the claims of religious com-
patibilities, real or imagined. We establish, on the
contrary, that the Africa, on behalf of whom reparations are sought, is that Africa that was enslaved
under the divine authority of the islamic and
christian gods, their earthly plenipotentiaries, and
commercial stormtroopers.

And next, the thesis of comparative humanism. We also come upon intensely argued apolo-
gia from some of our own African and African-
American scholars who inform us that the
condition of the slave under Arab slave-owners
was far more humane than under the European-
American. That may be demonstrable. Presum-
ably such research would involve, in the former
instance, only those who did survive the trans-
Saharan route; I do not imagine that evidence in
the form of extant engravings of slaves on the car-
avan routes, dying the slow death of thirst and
floggings, would bear this out, any more than the
clinical reports of losses by the merchant middle-
men. And I assume that the French would also
dispute such a thesis—at least where the female
slaves were concerned. To the French, slavery was
all very well but, in the territory of exotic libido
and its socialization—at least in those times—

there is no question that the black woman was in every way the equal, indeed the superior, of her white counterpart. The *signares* of Senegal, mistresses of French slavers, inaugurated a tradition of social acceptability that was even translated into French law, protecting the *café au lait* products and, indeed, guaranteeing unprecedented rights to the slave partner in such liaisons. From the *signare's* point of view, any claims to a greater degree of humanism by other slaving cultures than what she enjoyed under the French would be simply laughable. Equality in bed, backed by open domestic bliss, social acceptance, and French law? What more could a slave desire?

But—let the thesis stand. It simply seems to me rather presumptuous to offer absolution to the practitioner of a dehumanizing trade through an exercise in comparative degrees of abuse. In any case, we can leave that argument in the capable hands of the various revisionist schools of cliometrics—Fogel and company. And, to stir up those murky waters even more, hasn't the latest testifier, Keith Richburg, made a strong case for the opposing thesis? Such is the quality of blessing that he accords the deportation of his forebears, and their luck in being selected for the

55

American soil, that his recently published book, *Out of America*, just stops short of proposing that Thanksgiving Day should be shifted to the day that the African slave—hopefully his own direct ancestor—first set foot on American soil.

That of course is only one in the variety of weaponry in the arsenal that is mounted—directly or indirectly—against the battle for Reparations. Warped though Mr. Richburg's conclusions may be deemed, we must acknowledge as a valid corrective his endeavor to direct our attention to the cumulative effect of contemporary social mismanagement of the continent—a catalogue of disasters that owe their origin to human criminality, and thus lends persuasion to the position that the movement for Reparations is untenable because it has become—undeserved! Keith Richburg's contemptuous dismissal of the proponents of Reparations is one with which I confess more than a little sympathy—his book refers to Reparations only in passing, but it does provide a powerful critique that cannot be ignored. If we insist, on the one hand, that Reparations are—at the very least—a useful critique of Eurocentric historicism, we cannot, in all honesty, ignore the proposition that it also serves as a critique of African historicism. This latter is not an abstract issue, but an immediate, accusing reality. And this is why I, for one, can only express gratitude to Mr. Richburg for his searing indictment not only of a continent that has abandoned its humanity, but of his own countrymen and women for conduct that confers legitimacy on the inheritors of the external career of enslavement and thus obscures truthful apprehension of our history-in-the-making. Let the following passage serve as summation of our own bitterness and frustration at the thoughtlessness of our American relations—Mr. Richburg is narrating a familiar scene of uncritical hero-worshipping that has become the trademark of black American leaders at any encounter with the continent's leadership froth:

> When Strasser entered the meeting hall, sporting his now-trademark sunglasses and his camouflage battle fatigues, the crowd of mostly middle- and upper-class black Americans went wild with cheering, swooning from the women, some hoots and frenzied applause. Sitting in that hall, you might be forgiven for

thinking Strasser was a music celebrity, instead of a puny dictator. These black Americans were obviously more impressed with the macho military image Strasser cut than with the fact that he represents all that is wrong with Africa—military thugs who take power and thwart the continent's fledgling effort toward democracy. The chanting and hooting was a disgusting display, and to me it highlighted the complete ignorance about Africa among America's so-called black elite.

And where, by the way, is glamour-boy Strasser today?

Memory: Conflict and Healing

A people who do not preserve their memory are a people who have forfeited their history—words to that effect that I have adapted from Elie Wiesel and Danielle Mitterand. It is quite fitting therefore that UNESCO has committed itself to the preservation of the Slave Route, establishing a scientific committee to document, preserve, and

open up the landmarks of the Slave Route for pos-
terity. That, in itself, constitutes an act of reparation, will it or not—reparation is still reparation
by any other name! Long before this undertaking,
African-Americans made pilgrimages to the isle of
Goree, visited the forts and slave monuments of
Accra, Cape Coast, Dar es Salaam and Zanzibar,
traversed the tunnels and dungeons where their
ancestors had trodden, and agonized over what
gods they had failed to placate to bring down
such a calamity on their heads. I have myself par-
taken of such reminders, for these are as much a
part of our history, we, the stay-at-homes, a part
of our collective racial trauma as it is of those who
were forcibly displaced. But is that all it can be?
Should be? An evocation of trauma several centuries removed, an immersion in accusatory and
guilt-ridden history?

Every landmark is a testament of history, and
in our own indelible instance—from Goree
through the slave forts of Ghana to Zanzibar—
every fort and stockade, increasingly turned into
museums, is filled with grim evocations of this
passage of our history. They are indices of Truth,
an essence and a reality that offer any peoples,
however impoverished, a value in itself, a value

that, especially when rooted in anguish and sacrifice, may dictate a resolve for redemption and strategies for social regeneration. To act in any way that denigrates the lessons, the imperatives of that Truth, for demagogic or other opportunistic reasons, is to pollute a people's Source, and declare a new round of exterior control of a people's heritage. That last comment is inserted as a repeat of a warning, provoked by the demagogic and apparently influential black nationalist school of revisionism (earlier hinted at) in the United States that has tried to place the responsibility for our slavehood passage squarely in the camp of one racial group—the Jewish—through a singular feat of historic distortion, elision, and manipulation! Undeniably, within that convenient scapegoat group—and what racial group escapes intact from participation, at some commercial or ownership level or the other, in the degrading traffic?— records exist of individuals who indeed owned slaves and traded in them. But those who are embroiled in an anti-Semitic agenda should at least hold inviolate the authority of our shared history, not engage in distortions of provable reality for their private warfare. We have not yet even arrived at a unanimity over the viability of the project of reparations, yet here we have a tendency that is determined to divert the historic heritage of millions into futile cul-de-sacs of racial or political animosities and alliances. As a humanist, actively engaged for most of my mature existence in confronting all encroachments on the self-retrieval of my kind—and this centers on a truthful but critical embrace of our past—I find these games simply insulting to racial intelligence, and contemptuous of the humanity that exercises such intelligence.

It is not possible for us to ignore the actuality of brutal conflicts on our own continent—some as blatantly race derived as those between Senegal and Mauritania within this decade, and the even more intractable ongoing conflict in the Sudan, a conflict that has entailed over three decades of carnage, with the possible consequences of social disintegration of an enduring nature. The indigenous culture of Sudan is today imperilled as never before! Does this matter? Have we a duty to be concerned? Or threatened? Let us briefly digress and examine the general implications for the rest of the continent.

In consonance—a tragic oxymoron—still, in consonance with other contributory factors to

Africa's apparent destiny of instability, such as the yoke of colonial boundaries, there is this very issue of internal cultural retention, and a straining toward a reharmonization with the past. By this I mean simply that, if we succeeded in leapfrogging backward in time over the multiple insertions of the contending forces of dissension—be they of the West or the Orient, and with all their own mutually destructive schisms and fragmentations—if, by this process, we were able to regain a measure of anterior self-knowledge, it may be possible to regard religio-cultural interventions as possibly no more than disruptive illusions whose ramifications hold the future in thrall. In any case, how recent, in any effective way, were some of these intrusions? Of course, there is no suggestion here that the accretions of all such interventions be abandoned on all fronts, not in the least. One does not shed the scales of centuries as simply as a snake sloughs off its winter—or harmattan—skin. Our proposition is simply one of recollection, or, to go back to our commencing code, memory. The need for the preservation of the material and spiritual properties by which memory is invested. Acceptance of both its burdens and triumphs or—better still—its actuality, the simple fact of its anterior existence and its validity for its time. To accept that is to recognize the irrationality of mutual destructiveness on behalf of any values, any values whatsoever, however seductive—cultural, ideological, religious, or race-authenticated—that intervened and obscured or eroded those multiple anteriorities—of whatever kind—from which our being once took its definition.

These, for us, remain the warnings and lessons of the Sudanese conflict. In our own time, a culture is being raped, as if Africa had regressed to the battlefronts of the thirteenth and fourteenth centuries. There have been other less publicized but no less bloody race- and/or religion-inspired conflicts in other parts of the continent. We cannot sincerely address these sobering eruptions of a continent without recourse to the suspended questions of history, and without interrogating the agenda, disguised or overt, of those whose distortions of history prevent a proper apprehension of that history by the rest of the world, and especially among their own kind, their captive, impressionable audiences, seeking visible, identifiable targets for their immediate predicament or will to populist authority. Like it or not, imprecise and speculative though it may appear to those ensconced in the security of academia, the memory and vestiges of slavehood relations lie at the heart of a number of these conflicts, and until the enthronement of Truth, and the fulfillment of the imperatives of its recognition, the possibility of Reconciliation remains a chimera. Unlike the idealists of History, for whom History is an impersonal totem, a utopian projection thrust into the future by the unstoppable potency of some abstracted, extrapolated Will, and, nearer still, unlike the materialist (Marxist) revision of that persuasion, whose restitution of the human entity to history is no less reductive of that very entity, rendering it subservient to its own utopian vision, we insist on the determinant and purpose of history as the human entity in and for itself, even as asserted by W.E.B. Du Bois:

> It is easy for us to lose ourselves in details in endeavouring to grasp and comprehend the real condition of a mass of human beings. We often forget that each unit in the mass is a throbbing human soul....it loves and hates, it toils

and tires, it laughs and weeps in bitter tears, and looks in vague and awful longing at the grim horizon of its life....*

It would be false to claim that I recollected those words as I first stood on the beach of embarkation at Ouidah on the slave route but, unquestionably, there were such echoes in my mind, echoes of innumerable reminders of this most elementary truth of the human condition, one that does not permit the luxury, or indeed arrogance of abstractionist games in the quest for a humane order. Of all the landmarks of slavery that I had ever traversed, none, not even the grim tunnels of Goree or Cape Coast, worn smooth by the yet echoing slaps of feet on the passage into hell, could match the eerie evocation of the walk toward Embarkation Point on the coast of Ouidah, in the Republic of Benin, then known as the Kingdom of Dahomey. I keenly felt the inadequacy of words as I tried to set down what was

* W.E.B. Du Bois, *The Souls of Black Folk*, in *Three Negro Classics*, ed. John Hope Franklin (Avon Books, 1992).

clearly a collective experience of that day; still, the following did aspire to be a faithful record of the experience:

We traversed the actual route taken by the slaves on their way to embarkation, stood on the spot from which they cast their last look on homeland, over the grounds where thousands of the weak and the ill, and thus commercial handicaps, had been slaughtered and buried. We stood also on Suicide Point, where hundreds had broken their bonds and plunged to a kinder death than what the unknown threatened in their imagination. We visited slave museums, passed by the ancestral home of descendants of a notorious slave merchant, a Portuguese who had settled down to a polygamous existence, and fathered numerous mulattoes. We ran our fingers over antiquated cannons, metallic restrainers and other instruments of torture, passed over flagstones worn smooth by the boots of slave owners and the bare feet of slaves. In the museum were original sketches and water colours of slave bazaars, royal ceremonials at which slaves were ritualistically beheaded, open-air receptions for the officers of merchant vessels, scenes from slave raids and weepy embarkation scenes from which the artists, all Europeans, had attempted to extract the maximum pathos....

No experience however could match the long walk through clumps of mangrove and palms, with clutches of huts and palm frond encased compounds in pristine preservation, along the only safe path through treacherous marine ponds and mangrove swamps. As if by common consent, we breathed gently, as if we feared to disturb a somnolent air that had lain on the earth, seemingly undisturbed for centuries.... and so all the way to embarkation point, and the place of no return.

Those who knew only the dictionary meaning of pilgrimage experienced its essence that morning. It was sobering, reflective, and paradoxically devoid of all feelings of hatred, vengeance, not even indictment. There was only a quiescent residuum of history as palpable reality, as truth.*

Now, it is possible that there is something about the magnitude of some wrongs that transcends the feelings of vengeance, even of redress in any form. A kind of crimino-critical mass after which wrongs and suffering are transmuted into a totally different stage of sensibility from which can only derive a sense of peace, a space of Truth that overawes all else and chastens the human moral dimension. It is not a surrender to evil, not a condoning of wrongs; perhaps it is akin to a balm that comes after a cataclysm of Nature, even when clearly of man's making. It overrides grief and despair, diffuses rage, infuses one with a sense of purgation, the aftermath of true tragic apprehension.

...and to begin with, what humanity is—Slave?

Is this, however, the summative offering of such experience, an immersion in collective—and tran-

* "The Fictioning of Africa" (unpublished letter).

quilizing—trauma? Would this be the entirety of legacy in the preservation or evocation of memory? Jean Genet, invited to write a play for black actors—a challenge that resulted in *The Blacks*, responded with the question, "But what is black? And to begin with, what colour is it?" I believe that on the mound of slaughtered slaves, pulled downward into their resting place and suffused in their ancestral exhalations, an allied question must have raised itself in my mind: "But what is slave? And to begin with, what humanity is it?"

To speak of reparations, we have stressed, is to address the question: "on whose behalf?" And it seems a pointless question because the answer is, "on behalf of the enslaved." But what is *slave*? And to begin with, what humanity is it? What, precisely, is its ontology? Such questioning leads us inexorably to an almost murderous contestation with any refinements of distinction, such as the earlier mentioned sociological proposition that slavery under one dispensation—Arab or European—is to be preferred to slavery under another. Our variant on Genet's question implies, very simply, that this is a condition that is indivisible—except of course in sociological particulars—the house nigger versus the field nigger, etc.—the fact is that the ontology of *slave* (like water, light, lover, teacher, etc.) remains irrefrangible though plagued with ten to a thousand varieties. When we define that irrefrangible quotient, no matter how, we are confronted by an uncomfortable discovery, we move to identify the continuum of the slave *condition* even in the contemporary world—and I do not refer to the survival of slave markets, albeit outlawed by the United Nations, in some parts of the world. I refer to the condition—*slave*, the answer to the question: "to begin with, what is its humanity?" The answer to that question is: denial.

Now what is a denial of humanity? Fortunately, we can avoid controversy by simply citing illustrative certitudes. Do we wish to dispute that apartheid South Africa did correspond overwhelmingly to a denial of humanity? The condition of "slave" is a denial of the freedom of action, of the freedom of choice. Bondage, be it of the body or of the human will. We know that certain expressions are justly regarded today to have become victims of devaluation, victims of that vitiating affliction that renders a word flaccid from misuse: *slave* is a prime candidate, and most especially within societies that suffer from yet another affliction called political correctness.

Nevertheless, there is a psychological mutilation of the human entity that no other word appears to be able to capture. It is rendered palpable in the physical mutilation that is practiced in certain societies such as India—the mutilation of children in order to turn them into beggars, an odious, trans-border industry that has now come to the attention of human rights organizations. And, of course, we can hardly deny the reality of yet another slavehood industry—the sex slaves.

Nevertheless, there are house slaves and field slaves, and there are slaves in gilded cages and the world knows of others dangling on the gibbet, rotting on the magnolia tree. There are slaves as studs and slaves as victims of castration. There are married slaves and merely breeding slaves. And there are trusted slaves, keepers of their masters' purse, commercial representatives who travel long distances on their master's business and return to give dutiful account. There are the virtual spouses, the *signares* of Senegal, whose status was no less than that of mistress of the house. We have known slaves who, after manumission, aspire to and inherit the kingdom of their erstwhile masters, sometimes even acquiring slaves in turn. But they have never been masters of their own existence, nor have they plotted their own destiny. To expel this incubus that makes hunchbacks of their invisible being, they must first seize and alter that destiny. The leaders of the great slave revolts understood this. In any case, all *know* the slave condition, have been defined by it; it has entered the repertory of their self-cognition and years must be devoted to exorcising that portion of their being. One and all, from Booker T. Washington to the refurbished slave-Sultan or redeemed slave risen to the exalted rank of the Archbishop, to that one question—what is the humanity of slave?—they must answer: denial! Between pampered Ariel, with all his own magical powers, and the boorish Caliban, there is only a difference of taste—both remain slaves of Prospero, and Africa remains trapped in the nightmarish illusions of a Tempest.

With this recognition, can the project of reconciliation take root? Of course I do not speak of South Africa now, which has moved to throw off the shackles of slavery, but of the rest of the enslaved continent and its relay of slavemasters. No sooner is one fallen, than another, convinced that he has mastered the art of invulnerability, takes his place. This is what vitiates the campaign for Reparations for the slave experience. It is merely fortuitous, but indeed summatively symbolic, that the man at the heart of it all, Chief Moshood Abiola,* the President-elect of Nigeria, is today himself enslaved by one of the new breed of slave dealers, who actually boasts of power over the most heavily populated, most talented slave market that the African world has ever known. This mockery of history is complete even down to the underground railroad on which hundreds travel every day, this author included. Emissaries of this midget slavemaster, Sanni Abacha,† however, traverse the world in first-class comfort—at least to such places as still grant them audience—preening themselves as men of independent action, even conviction, but what in reality are they? Slaves into the twenty-first century, mouthing the mangy mandates of mendacity, ineptitude, corruption, and sadism. Never has impunity enjoyed such free reign as in the three years of the madness of Sanni Abacha's

* See note on page 45.
† See note on page 34.

dictatorship, the midget lord of the nation that launched a campaign for slavery reparations, and played such a glorious role in the ending of South Africa's apartheid slavery!

There was one other actor in that anti-slavery movement—his name is Olusegun Obasanjo. It was he who, as co-chairman with the former Prime Minister of New Zealand, led the Commonwealth Eminent Persons Group and broke down, for the first time, the barrier of Robben Island. Today,* he is held in some remote slave stockade of General Sanni Abacha, after a secret trial that, but for the then insecurity of the plantation master, would easily have ended as a lynching party. He earned a reprieve, but a certain group of scapegoats from a slave revolt did not. They were known as the Ogoni Nine, and, among them was a writer called Kenule Saro-Wiwa. Now that was a lynch party to beat the most gory escapades of the deep, Deep South. The world's memory may be short, but the world must never be permitted to forget *this*!

Truth, and Reconciliation. Is it possible that,

---

* Like most other victims of Sanni Abacha, General Olusegun Obasanjo has since regained his freedom.

one day, it will be sufficient for this particular anachronism of a slave-raider to drag his way onto a forum and, with the South African model as guide, confess to his crimes and be granted absolution? Or Mobutu Sese Seko? This strategy for social healing, we have stressed, is not, alas, taking place ahistorically. There is an ongoing context to such innovative tendencies and it is a context that constitutes its own worrisome critique. Or, let us put this differently, and with a more cogent summons, are certain aspects of these proceedings not in themselves a tarnishing of the quality of Truth and its imperatives and, thus, a condonation of impunity? For how else can one read an advance project of the remission of sins in the immediate context of the unfinished business of such criminality? The example of South Africa is not one that we dare recommend, untouched, for the travails of that continent, and for embarking on a process that will redress yet ongoing assaults against its humanity.

A Conditional Amnesty

It is surely a different social condition that validates the strategy for—shall we say—an amnesty for certain legal infractions that do not carry the burden of criminality. I refer, for instance, to the occasional call for a surrender of illegally possessed arms within a stipulated time. Amnesty is granted retroactively for that specific infraction, which presupposes that such arms have never been used in the commission of a crime. A recent example was the general acquisition of arms during the 1997 breakdown, not just of law and order, but of society in Albania. An intense phase of social anomie that rivalled, while it lasted, Somalia in the abyss of her own disintegration. Then there is looting, of which I happen to be able to narrate a lighthearted but fascinating and serendipitous instance, since the subject of our discourse does happen to be slavery.

The year was 1990, and I had been invited to Trinidad and Tobago's celebrations of her hundredth anniversary of Emancipation—the formal end of slavery. And Trinidad and Tobago, the land of rum and Coca-Cola, cricket, carnival, and calypso, just had to pick on that very occasion to join a very trendy post-colonial club. The sunshine island of Trinidad, at least, decided that she was entitled to a place in postmodern history by staging her very own coup d'état!

It would appear that a bunch of hare-brained adventurists, masquerading under a religious banner, had been training with some Mark IV rifles and the odd assault weapons in some equivalent of the American Freemen enclave. They finally moved to take over the House of Parliament during its session and to take the legislators hostage, announcing a change of government. The radio and television stations were also seized. Narrating the full details of that insolent parody of a coup d'état is much too tempting, so I had better not even attempt a résumé of it. Suffice it to say that, coming from a land where we live on a diet of coups for breakfast, lunch, and dinner—and yet end up with empty stomachs—I felt profoundly insulted to be caught in such a tawdry impudence of revolutionary aping and its accompaniment of illiterate bombast!

In the uncertain atmosphere that followed this coup, some Trinidadians went on a looting spree. The shopping centers were mostly left untouched—few were willing to venture that far from the security of their homes; no, it was the neighborhood stores that were broken into and looted. And this was what shocked the majority of the Trinidadians most. A few camera crews ventured out and some of the looters were caught on film. This did not seem to bother them—I suppose they thought it was simply a variation on the carnival. Television sets, stereos, refrigerators—some had succeeded in rustling up the odd car or utility truck to facilitate the exercise. Several of the shopkeepers were later interviewed—the shock on their faces and in their voices was most pathetic—and it was the usual story. Quite a number knew who the looters were; they had lived with them as neighbors for generations. This was the end of the world for them— they were quitting once the saga was over. Other Trinidadians were equally outraged or simply numbed with shock. An independent radio that had escaped seizure by the self-serving revolutionaries broadcast these tales of woe—the coup, it seemed, had unleashed the unsuspected beast of prey lurking in the easygoing calypso personality.

Well, after some three or four days of stalemate—and the personal indignity of being trapped on the island by a pack of cretinous dilettantes—the police got tired of the waiting game with the captors and their hostages and moved to at least save the community from itself. Taking advantage of the independent radio that had escaped seizure, the Chief of Police went on air and lectured the Trinidadians on their evil ways. Like a stern schoolmaster, he reminded them that this kind of act was unTrinidadian and warned that it would not be tolerated. Then he gave them all forty-eight hours to return the looted property. Just lay down your loot in front of your houses, he said; we will come round and collect them, and return them to their owners. No questions asked. Return your loot, and let Trinidad return to herself.

I drove round afterward with a friend. I could hardly believe my eyes. These goods were laid down neatly in front of houses. In some cases, looters who felt somewhat shamefaced—they appeared to cut across all classes—had asked neighbors to run the stuff over to the rightful owners. Some had apparently contacted their fellow felons and organized anonymous collective returns. Wheelbarrows were trundling through the streets in reverse directions, filled with clothing, toys, appliances, etc. The rum and beer were of course never recovered, but even the shopkeepers did not seriously expect to see such items restored to their shelves in undepleted forms. Something, after all, was needed to calm the nerves of a people during those tense days of the takeover of a nation.

Now, that was Trinidad. I tried hard to imagine the same scenario in my own native land of Nigeria. An appeal to return looted material? There would be picks and shovels in motion all night for temporary internment of stereos, refrigerators, and motorcycles. Rodents, wild fowl, and antelopes would find their repose rudely interrupted by the roar of looted motorcars crashing through their territory for temporary ensconcement!

But it was not always so. When a people have been continuously brutalized, when the language of rulers is recognized only in the snarl of marauding beasts of prey and scavengers, the people begin to question, mistrust, and then shed their own humanity and, for sheer survival, themselves become predators on their own kind. (This was the deduction that the Martiniquan psychiatrist, Frantz Fanon, also made from his studies in Algeria under a brutal French colonialism. What analysis, I wonder, would he make of the bestial violence inflicted on journalists, artists, and women, and other moslems deemed impure by the fundamentalist state-within-the-state of Algeria? And what manner of "Truth and

Reconciliation" proceeding could humanly accommodate the agents of a convinced divine mandate whose atrocities still have the capacity to shock even a world attuned to the Yugoslavian or Rwandan excesses?)

The real extract from our Trinidadian excursion, however, is the place of Restitution in the order of society. Yes, there was a general amnesty. A social aberration had taken place, which could easily, because of the circumstances, be extenuated. A contagious, temporary insanity. Even so, however, the general remission was conditional— restitution must first be made. This was the bedrock. If the fabric of society, ruptured by the double violence of the coup and the looting, was to be healed, there had first to be restitution. Truth alone is never enough to guarantee reconciliation. It has little to do with crime and punishment but with inventiveness—devising a social formula that would minister to the wrongs of dispossession on the one hand, chasten those who deviate from the humane communal order on the other, serve as a criterion for the future conduct of that society, even in times of stress and only then, heal. Memory—of what has been, of acts of commission or omission, of a responsibility abdicated—affects the future conduct of power in any form. Failure to adopt some imaginative recognition of such a principle merely results in the enthronement of a political culture that appears to know no boundaries—the culture of impunity.

A Millennial Reckoning?

Reparations therefore—as a condition of co-existence—cannot be faulted, and perhaps even South Africa, despite the ennobling authority of our authors, poets, and sages of forgiveness—William Conton *(The African)*, Léopold Senghor, Tierno Bokar *(The Sage of Bandiagara)*, James Baldwin *(Blues for Mr. Charlie)*, and all—may find that some formula is ultimately inescapable that will respond to the imperatives, the elementary justice of reparations. It should not be beyond the indicted group itself to respond to the heroic latitude of the victims by an equally heroic act of remorse, expressed in some ingenious way that encompasses, as we have stated, both the moral and the material, the latter of which can find realization in social constructs, clearly identified as such. Neglect of such a course provokes interpretation as vindication of the crime, a dangerous perception that, some unexpected day, may resurrect long dormant seeds of hate and resentment in the victim group. The race pathology of that erstwhile slave society, the United States of America, is a warning that is ignored at great peril.

As the world draws closer together—the expression "global village" did not come into currency for no just cause—it seems only natural to examine the scoresheet of relationships between converging communities. Where there has been inequity, especially of a singularly brutalizing kind, of a kind that robs one side of its most fundamental attribute—its humanity—it seems only appropriate that some form of atonement be made, in order to exorcise that past. Reparations, we repeat, serve as a cogent critique of history and thus a potent restraint on its repetition. It is not possible to ignore the example of the Jews and the obsessed commitment of survivors of the Holocaust, and their descendants, to recover both their material patrimony and the humanity of which they were brutally deprived. Attempts to insert an annulling distinction—such as time— between heirs to a crime against race—the Jewish as opposed to the black race, for instance—are filled with historic pitfalls and must be briefly touched on as we conclude. In any case, this can hardly be an exercise in competing interests, but a sincere interrogation of the project of reconciliation. The closeness to, or distance from, a crime whose effects are still recognizable in the present is no argument for or against the justice of reparations.

The practical implementations of the project of Reparations remain, of course, the most problematic, nearly daunting. Once, I proposed that the slaving nations simply annul the debts of the African world and we, in turn, would annul the incalculable injustice done to that world by today's beneficiaries of the slave commerce. Thus, we move into a new millennium with a slate wiped clean of the wounding accretions of the past. Indeed, we could then proceed to label our era the Century—or Millennium—of Global Annulment! The proposal did not appear to make much impression, I must confess, on the gathering of the hard-headed executives of the World Bank to whom it was addressed. From one point of view, such a proposal also appears unevenhanded, benefiting the improvident among African nations while shortchanging the prudent in economic management. The obvious response to this is that it was not governments that were enslaved in the first place, but peoples, and the peoples are far more sinned against (and by their own rulers past and present) than sinning. The material effect of the annulment of national debts is always imperceptible, in the short run, in the economic lives of a people, but it offers a chance for a new beginning, terminates a recurrent excuse employed by governments for the neglect or collapse of development, and, ideally, stiffens the resolve of the governed in their demand for the practice of accountability. Essentially, however, it carries with it a hands-across-the-divide global comprehensiveness in our quest for the resolution of a bitter passage of our interlocked histories. Also—encroaching now on another course that is being pursued by UNESCO as well as national and private campaigners as an autonomous moral objective—so would the return of a major part of the looted artistic treasures of a continent, now secured in European national museums, to their original homes. The arts are, after all, the material expression of a people's humanity; they can play a more than symbolic role in reconciling, with their violators, a people whose humanity has been so comprehensively denied.

We remind ourselves yet again that the internal slavery currently inflicted on a continent's surviving millions by their own kind renders moot the entire notion of reparations—can any argument from the throat of a Mobutu Sese Seko or Sanni Abacha carry any conviction in a universal court of equity? I, for one, decline in advance to have my interests conflated with such proven collaborators in the slavehood enterprise. For us, in these dire times, reparations, like charity, should begin at home, and the wealth of the Mobutus, the Babangidas, the Abachas, but also the de Beers, Shell Surrogates Incorporated, etc. of the continent should be utilized as down payment, as evidence of internal moral cleansing, that would made any claims for worldwide reparations irreproachable. Reparations would therefore involve the acceptance by Western nations of a moral obligation to repatriate the post-colonial loot salted away in their vaults, in real estate, business holdings, and cover ventures by those African leaders who have chosen to follow the European precedent in the expropriation of a continent. The plunder could never have been possible, would never have reached such mammoth proportions, without the collaboration of those same commercial centers of Europe and, lately, the wealthier Arab nations. So let this be a concerted, preliminary step in Reparations—an act that acknowledges the guilt of accessories and makes restitution to the victims of the principals. Rigorously pursued, the recovered fortunes will provide a breathing space directly to the distressed economies of those countries that have been pillaged by their incontinent leaders. An embarrassed Swiss government and its banks are currently engaged in such an exercise on behalf of the victims of the Jewish Holocaust—it is both a project of restitution and a self-purgation of long-denied fascist complicities, now bared naked to the world.

We remain conscious of, and must build on, our heritage of glories, but the self-inflicted passages of ignominy remain to also indict our present. The scenes of African slave lords decapitating their own kind for the delectation of officers from slave ships provide some of the most chastening images, for us, in the archives of slavery—and of course even our oral history provides unambiguous testimonies on the fatal delinquency of our own kind. The conduct of traditional rulers in thrall to new military enslavers is a bitter *reprise* of our history. Nigeria, as always in the forefront of such obscenities, is again crisscrossed today by the sycophantic trails of slime along which crawl the erstwhile majesties of obis, obas, and emirs in homage to the new slavemasters in military uniform. One after the other they slither and slide, tumble over one other, grapple with one another by the trail of their robes and royal sceptres in an effort to be first at the ritual of self-abasement at the feet of some unripened thug with a swagger-stick. The tradition of withdrawal and seclusion in the face of superior forces is abandoned, as are their people, for the brief replenishment from contracts and preferments. Not for them the silent symbol whose *absence* speaks volumes, and infuses resistance with more than mystic blessing.

Are these the kings of whom the griots sang? Are these their descendants? We do not know them, but we know from which lines—between those who resisted and those who fawned on the presence of their enslavers—the majority of these are descended. We know the difference between

Oba Ovheramwen, whose defiance of the British led to the sacking of Benin in the eighteenth century, and the present incumbent of his throne. Ile-Ife, the cradle of the Yoruba people, indeed of the black races of the world, is today an alms house tenanted by a mendicant who surely makes his ancestors drown the heavenly rafters with their tears. If, in a freak teleological reversal, the world were to follow Napoleon's example and reinstate slavery after its abrogation—perhaps our planet is invaded, and the United Nations is subjected to a new definition of humanism by superbeings from outer space?—we recognize among us those who would be first in line to offer up their own kith and kin; their genealogy is branded on their foreheads like the mark of Cain.

The righteous armor of demand for ancient wrongs is thus sadly dented. The ignominious role of ancient rulers, continuing into the present, serves to remind us of their complicity in the cause for which reparations are sought. Without their collaboration, with, on the contrary, due commitment to the protection of their kind, the slave trade would have been stemmed at its source. Even if the African continent had been devastated as a consequence...well, why speculate? We only know that the continent *was* devastated by their choice, and that their complicity, echoed today in the politics of power, clouds what should have been a clear division between victim and violator. Nevertheless, the principle of recompense can be elicited both from objective criteria and from the regard of the European and Asian worlds toward their own histories. We cannot dismiss a process that boasts the virtue of calling a flawed historicism into question, and enables us to criminalize the internal continuum of an external violation. And let this point be stressed for the instruction of dismissive voices on this subject: negating arguments based on the antiquity of the collective injustice of slavery do not vitiate the principle. From Australia through Japan to the United States: President Clinton's apology—preceded by reparations—to the black victims of the scandalous syphilis experimentation; the commemoration and rehabilitation of the victims of the 1692 Salem witchhunt; Japanese apology and compensation fund for Korean "comfort women" —yes indeed, the world does appear to be caught up in a *fin de millénaire* fever of atonement. The African demand for reparations precedes this fever; however, it is not part of any bandwagon effect. And this universal mood of reckoning appears to observe no statute of limitations. A surely antiquated wrong against Spanish jewry— just one final example!—the 1492 edict of Ferdinand and Isabella that evicted Jews from Spain—was redressed only last year by the Spanish government. Export of the first slave from the West African coast predated this by only fifty years, and the full-blown European entry into the commerce did not begin until the seventeenth century, continuing, in some instances, well into the late nineteenth century. Slavery itself was not abolished in Brazil and parts of the Caribbean until the last decade of that same century. Which of these memories, then, least deserves the peace of amnesia? How come that a five-centuries-old "crime against humanity" committed against the Jewish race has not been relegated to the archives of lapsed injustices? Is it nothing but idle compulsion that drives humanity to exhume and atone for past crimes against its kind? And is the African world then, yet again, of another kind, one that is beneath the justice of atonement and restitution? Justice must be made manifest either for all, or not at all.

*   *   *

We shall award the (albeit indicted) European humanities the last word in this charter of claims on behalf of memory. If we may appropriate Shakespeare's words in a context that, however inelegant, I am certain the Bard would approve of, we say of the blindfolded beauty that is Justice: "Age cannot wither her. Nor custom / Stale her infinite variety." Within that infinite variety, we may seek pragmatic answers for the modalities of a marriage of the two contending tendencies that will produce a healing millennial trilogy: Truth, Reparations, and Reconciliation.

II

L.S. Senghor and Negritude

J'accuse, mais, je pardonne

Léopold Sédar Senghor, scholar, statesman, politician, and poet extraordinaire, was ninety in September 1996. Some insist he was actually ninety-three, but records at that time make Senghor's age rather speculative. Under the auspices of UNESCO, along with the French and Senegalese governments, a truly impressive array of scholars, politicians, artists, and friends were brought together in Paris to pay him tribute. I was privileged to participate in this event, which could not help but be both a celebration and reassessment of the life and achievements of this controversial scholar and poet, as well as a retrospective of his times. It was an occasion that lent itself to a convenient dichotomy that governed the themes of the two main sessions: Senghor the politician, and Senghor the poet and scholar. Of course, the complex territories traversed by the numerous papers indicated quite early that these divisions were merely convenient categories. Even the celebrant's own contribution to the proceedings suggested that there was yet another facet of his complex personality that deserved some attention. I identify it as: Senghor the priest and evangelist.

And that sense of assertion by a neglected category came about this way. Mr. Senghor was himself unable to be present at his own anniversary because of the constraints of age, so the camera invited us into his home, followed him into his study, and explored with him the calm of a beautifully manicured garden. It was not a garden filled with the tamarind trees of Joal, the perfumes it gave off would clearly not be "of the bush, hives of russet bees that dominate the crickets"; it was simply the clipped grounds and luxuriant flowers of his obviously French country home, his French wife by his side, in an ambiance that was clearly alien to the majority of—shall we simply say?—the Senegalese who, in far off West

Africa, were similarly gathered to do him honor. That ambiance was one that had shaped his sensibilities both as thinker and poet, despite his undeniable fidelity to the absent sources from whose darker, ancestral draughts he also, as thinker and poet, drank. As if those immediate outward images with which we were confronted were not, however, sufficient to narrate the full inner biography of this remarkable man, he proceeded to bare his thoughts from within that cherished influence to his distant audience through a filmed address. It had a rather wistful, valedictory tone in the circumstances, resurrecting, in one of those strange flashbacks, a long receded image—straight from my student days: a frail figure by a staircase, an operatic baritone singing *Guten Abend* during a Christmas telecast—just one of those instant flashes that superimpose themselves on an actuality. I believe it was Tito Gobbi, and I recollect that he had forced himself out of a sickbed to participate in that broadcast.

No matter, Senghor's address—as impeccably phrased, though less lyrical than the Tito Gobbi performance his frailness evoked—was one that summed up his cultural conviction, a by now familiar brand of humanism that took, as its basis, a distinct, indeed a near unqualified commitment to European—and specifically—French culture. It reminded us all of the fact that there always was one undeniable quality to Senghor's lifelong response to his colonial, Gallic encounter— consistency. If any of us had come to that gathering thinking that there would be a winter conversion, a re-examination of what—to many of us— had always appeared an unnecessary philosophical accommodation of, an assimilative creative response to a colonial, indeed, imperial culture, we were doomed to be disappointed. And therein lay, I suspect, the core of what had always appeared troublesome to those of us who, right from our brash creative youth, rejected the banner of Negritude as a philosophy of immediate relevance to our colonial and post-independence realities. Even then, however, in those early days, there was a niggling suspicion in the mind, indeed, one that was often implicit in the very language and focus of rejection in the turbulent sixties, that it was not so much the message that was contested as the messenger himself, both as medium and mediator.

The really absorbing exercise today therefore in reviewing the career of Senghor lies probably in the attempt to reinterpret the messenger himself, an exercise that is made easier if one recollects that, like Martin Luther King, whose anniversary is now registered worldwide on the calendar, Léopold Sédar Senghor was a priest—but a failed one. This is a fact of his life that is not often recollected, or given its full significance. And when I say failed, I do not mean that he tried and failed; no, simply that this was the one half of his ambition of which he was deprived quite early— Senghor, on his own admission, wanted to be a professor and a priest. And my suspicion is that he never quite gave up that latter inclination, which is hardly surprising. Janet Vaillant* provides an illuminating and moving account of the young Senghor's intense depression when his expectations for the furtherance of his chosen career—to proceed to the seminary—were frustrated. Senghor returned to his native Joal, refused to be comforted, "would not go out of the house but hid in the dark." He likened himself to "a defrocked priest," and complained that the church had rejected him. His destiny was to

* Janet A. Vaillant, *Black, French, and African* (Harvard University Press, 1990).

become a soldier (drafted into service), a teacher, a politician, a poet, and scholar, but Léopold Sédar Senghor truly had this priestly avocation, and his poetry and essays are filled, I propose, with compensatory tracts for that missed, and probably envied calling.

This is why I have subtitled this essay, "I accuse, but I forgive." And like Martin Luther King, this capacity to forgive the enemy is also based on love—at least a certain doctrine of love. Reading King's letter from the Birmingham jail to his fellow prelates, it is not too difficult to experience the same sensation of a spiritual agonizing as one finds embedded in Senghor's "Prayer for Peace" from his long, self-unravelling poem, *Hosties Noires* (Black Host), written early in his career. The central imagery, the significance of the eucharist—but this time, a black version—that is introduced in the title is of course deliberate—it is christian and Roman Catholic. It provokes the equation of the black race to the object of sacrifice, and does so in a context that places nations that profess christianity in the dock of humanity. But not for long, not without the assurance of redemption. To ensure, absolutely, that we do not miss the christian foundation for this message of forgiveness, Senghor even prefaces the poem with the relevant section of The Lord's Prayer, and in the original Latin of the Roman Catholic service—*Sicut et nos dimittimus debitoribus nostris* (forgive us our trespasses, as we forgive them that trespass against us). The informing urge is always toward forgiveness, toward the remission of sins.

Since Martin Luther King was a professed and practicing minister, there is really nothing special to remark in the fact that, in his justly famous *Letter from Birmingham City Jail,* he takes pains to recall his fellow ministers to the fact that *"Jesus Christ was an extremist in love...and thereby rose above his environment."* It is the difference in the rhetorical strategies and summative intent of these two that strikes one forcibly, and provokes astonishment, for Martin Luther King, the advocate of nonviolence, was actually turning his critics' position on its head. They denounced his actions—his Civil Rights strategies of *peaceful* confrontation—as unchristian and extremist. Martin Luther King employed the same canons of the christian faith to justify, indeed extol, the virtues of certain forms of extremism. It would be stretching the boundaries of the word much too far to even suggest that, in his own mode of denunciation of the evils of colonialism or racism, Léopold Senghor ever came close to being an extremist. His contemporary kindred spirit—but only in the significance of one concluding event, not the process of struggle itself—is perhaps South Africa's Bishop Desmond Tutu, the moving spirit behind the Truth and Reconciliation Commission.

This striking contrast between Martin Luther King and Senghor is what constitutes the element of disquiet for even the most ardent of the devotees of Senghor's lyrical mastery. For those whose historic consciousness is rooted in the plain fact of being victims of racial—and colonial—oppression, it is a quality of accommodativeness that is near incomprehensible. Martin Luther King's "love" is more accessible. It is grounded in a near universal foundation of community, of humanity, even though its expression is decidedly christian—Tierno Bokar's faith *(The Sage of Bandiagara)* in the reconciliation of races and faiths is elicited through a similar embrace that commences with the islamic faith, a "love" that expands, like King's, into a universal redemption for humanity. It is a love that is affirmed within a humanistic framework, indeed, one that defines humanism as

an affirmation of community when based on tolerance and love. Senghor's is selectively nationalistic (and by adoption!), a poet's special advocacy
that seeks to universalize a specific civilization and
culture.

Not that Senghor was unconscious of the
cruelties of nations whose credo supplies the
foundation of that same christian love indeed,
he has confessed to a loss of faith for about a year
in direct response to the contradictions and racist
inhumanities of the white nations, France most
directly. This rupture of his romance with France
was starkly expressed in the lines:

I shall tear the banana laughter from all
   the walls of France

Forward! And may there be no song of
   praise O Pindar! But shaggy

> *war shout and quick sword thrust!*
>   (*"A l'Appel de la race de Saba"*)

The language of such lines makes for rare encounter, however, and, of course, Senghor is
saved from the abyss by the same virtue of love—
for France and humanity. This is not unusual; the

profession of love is one that we encounter among embattled leaders and thinkers of varied religious persuasions—as a controlling weapon of conflict—Ghandi, Nelson Mandela, James Baldwin, etc. In that same letter from Birmingham jail, for instance, Martin Luther King makes this personal avowal in the face of abandonment (or repudiation) by the establishment guardians of the faith: "Yes, I love the church; I love her sacred walls. How could I do otherwise? I am in the rather unique position of being the son, the grandson, and the great-grandson of preachers. Yes, I see the church as the body of Christ."

The conflation of this christian advocacy with the elevation of the human spirit, communal responsibility, and dignity, proposed as a right and a *duty*, then appropriates and directs the secular world of human relationships and becomes the principal *argument* in Martin Luther King's address, moving persuasively along the very parameters that have been misappropriated by his adversaries as "rational" curbs on his commitment, on his sense of immediacy. The genius of Martin Luther King lay in his intelligent seizure of the high moral ground on the very fields of disputation introduced by his adversaries—*law* or *time*, for instance. King dismisses all propositions of the neutrality of time in regard to the tempo of struggle, reminding his critics of its convenient appropriation for good or evil by contending social forces. And he deploys a shared christian theology to buttress his own political recourse to the very foundation of law as expounded by christian theologians: "I would agree with Saint Augustine" declares the Rev. King, "that an unjust law is no law at all." And King proceeds to define his position on what is just and unjust as law. "A just law" he proposes,

> is a man-made code that squares with the moral law or the law of God. An unjust law is a code that is out of harmony with the moral law. To put it in the terms of Saint Thomas Aquinas, an unjust law is a human law that is not rooted in eternal and natural law. Any law that uplifts human personality is just. Any law that degrades human personality is unjust.

Senghor would hardly disagree; the question that is posed by his theology of accommodativeness is: what is to be done (or, more relevantly in his case, poetized) where the just law has been broken or ignored, continues to be broken and defied, where the unjust law continues to be observed in relationships between communities and races? And what is to be done with memory? Must memory be a casualty (or sacrifice) of time? Where the material of memory is active in the present, holds sway in the iniquitous present, where precisely lies the priestly (or poetic) duty?

The Quality of Mercy Is—Strained?

Now, before we get carried away by comparisons, let us recall that a poet's mission is quite different from that of an activist minister of God, especially one who is involved in establishing the rule of law (or of God) in the secular world. The poet operates wherever necessary, even through self-cancelling strategies—hyperboles, condensation, ellipsis, obliqueness, etc., leaping over rational ramparts to seduce and convert, while the minister here, engaged in the seizure and application (or repudiation) of precepts, is as punctiliously expositional as time—of which he had plenty—indulged him. They do, however, share the common platform of rhetoric, but while one wrestles (in the manner of Saul and the angel) with his opponent, the other appears to be already within his embrace. Unlike King, Senghor is not appealing for active and immediate redress from the conscience of the oppressor; he does not express his state of being as one within the cauldron of an ongoing struggle, demanding something that is being withheld. Senghor appears compelled to quarry deep into the humanism of the oppressed to escape the undeniable pressure of history, counter its imperatives in the present with an excursion into pristine memory, and forge, from within its purity and innocence, an ethos of generosity whose lyrical strength becomes its main justification.

We are therefore obliged to limit ourselves to just one element—the "quality of mercy" of both protagonists—this is what we may usefully extract and contrast—and the use to which both have put a shared community of faith and the articles of that faith on which the principle of forgiveness may derive its authority. I love the church, says one, and the church preaches love—and, on that basis, my actions must be based on love, and thus I shall transcend my environment. The other launches a prayer-poem for the forgiveness of the enemy, pleading—yes, admittedly—I also seek to transcend that environment of hate, but most intrusively—*Car j'ai une grande faiblesse pour la France* (for I have this great weakness for France). However disarming we may adjudge such candor, it is difficult not to respond with the censure of an artistically affronted Hamlet: "What is Hecuba to him, or he to Hecuba?" In Yoruba, this would translate as "being guilty of dyeing one's mourning robes a deeper indigo than the cloth of the bereaved." Can we, however, go so far as to allege—and Lilyan Kesteloot* is a persuasive advocate to the contrary—that "Senghor made peace with the West over the dead bodies of his victimised race"? Only if we fail to accept the panhumanistic vision of Senghor, which also insists that "charity begins at home" and makes the uncharitable its first beneficiary.

What gets in the way of Senghor's panhumanistic pleading is the identification of a redeemed son among the prodigals—and not even on the authority of the unambiguous expression of contrition, but simply by virtue of a "unique" history and culture. The attractiveness of the social manifesto of the French Revolution,

* Lilyan Kesteloot, *Black Writers in French* (Temple University Press).

its rousing appeal of *fraternité* and *égalité*, can only be regarded as a partial, and still unsatisfactory, explanation. Today, we are inclined to recognize in Senghor the poetic anticipation of South Africa's Truth and Reconciliation Commission.

The initiators of that process of healing, however, do not permit the remotest suggestion of a concession of the superiority of their oppressor—moral, scientific, or cultural—any more than does Martin Luther King, or the majority of the Negritude poets, even of Senghor's own generation. There is something that generates both intellectual and visceral unease in what can only be interpreted as endorsement of the aggressor's claims to superiority, that common basis for a historic relegation of *the other* to a subhuman status. It is intolerable enough when these claims are made by the "superior" race itself. When laudatory lines by the victim enhance such claims, it resounds like a poetic kiss of absolution on the ring on the whiphand. Here is the context of that cited declaration of love for France:

Lord God, forgive white Europe!
It is true, Lord, that for four centuries of

enlightenment she threw her foaming,
yelping dogs upon my lands
And that Christians, in denial of Your
word and mildness of Your heart
Lit their campfires with my parchments,
put my seminarians to torture, sent
my doctors and my learned men to
exile....

Lord, forgive those who made guerrillas
of the Askias, who turn my princes
into sergeants
Made houseboys of my servants, and
labourers of my country folk, who
turned my people into a proletariat
For you must forgive those who hunted
my children like wild elephants
Who trained them to the whip and made
them the black hands of those whose
hands were white
You must forget those who stole ten
millions of my sons in their leprous
ships
And who suppressed two hundred million
more

(*"Hosties Noires"*)

So far then—and this is the informing structure of this incantatory poem—we find ourselves inducted into an ironic antiphony, a bill of indictment countering a charter of forgiveness. We are kept firmly within the territory of a magnanimity that does not, however, gloss the catalogue of wrongs. But then what to make of France's exceptional status? It does not proceed from the *history* of the behavior or character of the excepted race, not as some form of conduct that is *demonstrated* to us as a contrasted moral superiority to others, not from any extenuating circumstances in the relationship of such a race to the aggrieved. France, it would appear, is exceptionally blessed simply from the privilege of being itself! Indeed, in this instance, the historic material of her conduct, the material by which we can judge or assess the claims of such a nation to an "exempt status," is demonstrably a betrayal of its own much vaunted humanistic ethos. The "egalitarianism" that is inscribed on the French national flag was an egalitarianism of cruelty and inhumanity at par with other slaving and colonizing nations on the one hand—no better and no worse—and on the other, a denial of that same egalitarian virtue to the black race.

Therefore, it is with a sense of bewilderment, unprepared and resentful, that we find ourselves in that special territory of the manumission of sins, inhabited by that one nation at the head of other collaborators in deeds of damnation. It was not simply a question of history, of the past and the indictment of memory. The actualities that led to the creation of Negritude were palpable and existed in the present continuous. Their articulation was not restricted to the poet in the artist, or the polemicist and universalist within the ranks of Marxist visionaries and utopians. It was a *lived* actuality, both on the African continent of René Maran, the black (French) administrator of Ubangi-Shari (despite the repulsive exotica of his fictionalized testimony, *Batouala*) and within the Caribbean, such as the Guadaloupe of Catyce or the Guyana of Léon Damas, whose response to his return to his native island as part of a research mission by the French Museum of Ethnography was summed up in his report, *Retour de Guyane*. Whatever anthropological exotica the Museum had hoped he would unearth, the unwelcome result was a searing sociological indictment of French colonial policies on his native island and its consequences on the populace. France, he claimed, had reduced Guyana to a "cesspool," and for no other purpose but the protection of her own national health. These were all artist-intellectuals whose activities closely intertwined; together, they were the midwives of Negritude.

Worth quoting for its own sake—frankly irresistible—is the following passage from France's own conception of her civilizing mission, written about the same time as Léon Damas' studied *J'Accuse*. This passage formed part of an introduction to an anthology *L'Homme du couleur*, dedicated—no less—to providing a vocal platform for the black intelligentsia. Even Senghor felt obliged to counter, albeit with studied, "diplomatic tact" (Lilyan Kesteloot), such libelous condescension in his own contribution, *Ce que l'homme noir apport*. That racism can be sometimes more dehumanizing and degrading through pietistic utterances than from even physical brutalization is amply demonstrated in Cardinal Verdier's statement of mission:

Nothing is more moving than this gesture of the Frenchman, taking his black brother by the hand and helping him to rise. This hierarchic but nonetheless real

111

collaboration, this fraternal love stooping toward the blacks to measure their possibilities of thinking and feeling; this gradual initiation to all the sciences and arts; this care that the natives should not be too suddenly removed from their milieu, their habits and traditions; this art, in a word, of helping them progress through wise development of their personality toward an improved physical, social, and moral well-being; this is how France's colonizing mission on the black continent appears to us! May this work of colonization maintain its purity, its respect for human personality, its truly fraternal love inspired by that most Christian idea of the fundamental equality of all races and the divine essence of all men!

May it continue carefully to avoid what has so odiously been called "man's exploitation of man."

Accepting Cardinal Verdier's sanctimonious treacle at exactly its face value—that is, examining the recordbook of French colonial mission in the light of this ennobling injunction, especially its avoidance of "man's exploitation of man"—it is a little taxing to comprehend Senghor's plea for France's special status on Judgment Day:

> *Lord, among the white lands, set France*
> *upon the Father's right hand*

Our route to Senghor's inhuman heart of forgiveness—yes, inhuman, because near super-human, transcendental—becomes easier perhaps if we recognize in him the Father Confessor who seizes the poetic privilege of presuming the confession of his sinners, treats their *mea culpa*s as already intoned, then grants them absolution. Yet here again, he refuses to stay detached. The poet places himself on the rack, aspires to the superhumanity of a Christ on the cross, overcoming the mortal instinct toward a hatred or rejection of the enemy. That "hate," that renunciation, becomes the enemy to be overcome, not the aggressor, not the slaver's own hatred or disdain toward the victim. The nearer the origination of hurt, the tighter must be the embrace, so that the most deserving of hate in the poet's own narrated experience— France—must be accorded a special place at the confessional, where the victim's generosity is made almost a condition of that same victim's humane restoration.

It is possible to toy with this generous view because Senghor is not alone in this regard among the poets of wrongs and suffering. If you take the war poets, for instance, those exposed to the brutality and dehumanization of war—Wilfred Owen, Siegfried Sassoon, Rupert Brooke, etc.—the residual sensibility is the same. Overwhelmed by the sheer immensity of suffering, or immersed in—to cite Hannah Arendt—the "banality of evil,"—it is pathos, or a somber harmony, that becomes the primary poetic extract. Is it of any significance that Senghor had also been a soldier and prisoner? That he had seen combat, albeit briefly, and absorbed—if only by self-transposition—the awful immensity of the instant voids of existence where once comrade and enemy stood? And no one need be astonished that Senghor's humanity expresses its love—and optimism in its capacity for transformation—for both victim and aggressors, conquerors and the conquered in such lines as the following:

> Neither masters any more nor slaves nor
>   knights nor griot of griots
> Nothing but the smooth and virile

> *camaraderie of battles*
> *And may the son of the captive be my*
> *equal*
> *the Moor and Targui, those congenital*
> *enemies, my companions!*
>
> *("A l'Appel de la race de Saba")*

Such lines, like the rejection of differentiation, the humane empathy in the works of the cited war poets, do not, however, glorify the enemy, only portray them as comrades caught in the vice of a universal irrationality. The combatants meet on a level playing field. The "serpent of hate" that such poets successfully overcome in their hearts has not been hatched from the denial of humanity by one side to the other, and the continuing relegation of the latter to a subhuman status, even away from the fields of slaughter. There were—and we shall come to them—other Negritude poets who constantly battled this tension between hate and the healing that forgiveness accords, but they did not exactly place themselves as such superhuman advocates for the prerogative of mercy.

> *And the serpent Hatred stirs his head*
> *within my heart, the serpent I'd*
> *thought dead....*

Kill it Lord, for I must proceed upon my
    way, and strangely, it is for France I
    want to pray,
Lord, among the white lands, set France
    upon the Father's right....

Yes Lord, forgive France, who expresses
    the right way so well, and makes her
    own so deviously....

Oh Lord, dismiss from my memory the
    France that is not France, this mask
    of pettiness and hate upon the face of
    France
The mask of pettiness and hate for which
    I've only hate—but surely I can hate
    the evil
For I am greatly fond of France.

Yes indeed, the confession of a strange—one would almost say, perverse—love affair whose celebration runs right through not merely "Prayer for Peace" but much of Senghor's poetic advocacies. The ardor had clearly not abated in the nonagenarian as he faced the cameras and dictated his poetic and philosophical testament to critics and admirers wherever they might be. It was the hour of summative benediction, the final act of the anointment that commenced in *Prayer for Peace* where, whatever blemishes the poet could not objectively ignore were presented—unlike those that belonged to other nations that stood equally indicted—as *not* being the real face of France. They are "masks" of hate and pettiness. The real France, for Senghor, is the France that "expresses the right way so well"; it is the France that has made "these daytime slaves into men of liberty, equality, fraternity." And so, upon that France, and her scholars, educators, colonial servants, and missionaries, Senghor expends his appropriated powers of priestly blessings:

> *Bless these people who brought me Your*
> *good tidings, Lord, and opened my*
> *heavy eyelids to the illumination of*
> *Your faith*
> *And opened my heart to knowledge of the*
> *world, bringing me a rainbow of new*
> *brothers*

Only toward the end does the Senghor of the mid-forties appear to recall that, specifically, the invaded, the transgressed, and the oppressed themselves could do with a bit of blessing:

And with them bless all of Europe's
people, Asia's, Africa's and America's

No wonder even Senghor's championship of the
cause of African spirituality and its inclusion in the
inventory of victims becomes suspect—is this
merely a convenient part of the antiphonal motif
of wrongs and forgiveness, or is the poet truly
assaulted by the fate of the African deities when
he accuses:

> *Oh! more than one of your Messengers,*
> *I know, tracked down my priests like*
> *animals and destroyed our sacred*
> *images*

For a convinced Roman Catholic and near
priest—despite a brief "loss of faith"—it reads
suspiciously like a symbolic effort at ecumenical
embrace, recalling the unkind and—surely—mis-
conceived comment by the poet and critic Felix
Morisseau-Leroy on yet another of the Negritude
poets, Léon Damas, on his death:

> When I listened to him, I closed my eyes
> and imagined some very progressive,
> very talented white French scholar *with*

*a favourable prejudice toward the negro point of view on problems of creative arts or history"** (my emphasis).

Vaillant's† query is justly posed. "It is noteworthy," she writes, "that the poet never suggests that his christianity may be one of his sins against his ancestors. Why should they not be jealous of his worship of an alien god?" Fortunately, successive waves of powerful, liturgical invocation of ancestral images, creating a sense of sincere veneration throughout Senghor's poetry, testify to the contrary. The love of Senghor for these sources and his attribution of deep humanistic lessons to them (both in their own right and as critique of occidental values), effectively counter such suspicions. It is not possible to question the force of Senghor's belief in this "Negritude of the source" as expressed at every opportunity, such as in the following passage:

> In Black Africa, any work of art is at the same time a magic operation. The aim is

* *The Gleaner's Sunday Magazine*, March 12, 1978.
† Vaillant, op. cit.

to enclose a vital force in a tangible cas-
ing, and, at the appropriate moment,
release this force by means of dance or
prayer.*

Is it, however, just our own imperfect humanity
that accepts on the one hand, Senghor's evocations of the moral virtues of a continent, elicited
from history, social usage, relationships, and art,
in the cause of spiritual self-affirmation, in distinct
distantiation from the West, but balks at the evocation of the virtues of the same source in the
cause of forgiveness and the generosity of
embrace?

Tchikaya U'Tamsi, the Congolese poet, also
an occasional apostle of reconciliation, at least
makes his capacity for forgiveness contingent on a
preliminary—and implicitly undesired—exercise
in self-induced amnesia. Lines from a poem following the murder of Emmet Till:

And I,
I forget to be Negro in order to forgive

---

* L.S. Senghor, *L'Art negro-africaine,* cited in Kesteloot.

No longer will I see my blood upon their
  hands
it's sworn....

Enough of this scandal on my life
I'll no longer see my blood upon their
  hands
I forget to be Negro to forgive the world
  for this

Or his imprecations against that Christ in whose
name (or under whose authority, within whose
"kingdom of this world") such deeds are permitted:

Christ, I spit on your joy,
The sun is black with suffering Negroes
With dead Jews searching for the leaven
  for their land

What do you know of New Bell?
At Durban two thousand women,
At Pretoria two thousand,
At Kin as well two thousand
And at Ansirabe two thousand more.
What do you know of Harlem?
              (*"The Scorner—Viaticum"*)

Like Senghor's, a bill of indictments, but without the compromises, without the attenuating threading for historic wrongs. Tchikaya U'Tamsi shares with Aimé Césaire the same temperament that stamps criminalities on their source, and questions the social foundations—in religion or philosophy—of their perpetrators. Tchikaya does not hesitate—albeit in the anguished accents of a lapsed adherent—to apportion blame to a failed deity, accuse him of betrayal or, at least, neglect.

During the Paris celebrations, my mind returned again and again to such numerous contrasts to the early poems of Senghor—*Hosties Noires* was first published in 1945—and I found myself increasingly obliged to confront, on its own terms—for the first time, it must be admitted—the centrality that the creed of *forgiveness* occupies in his works—forgiveness, that is, as a universe of its own, a universe that must be negotiated by sensibilities that have been shaped by forces that are alien to the majority of mankind. And this was probably due to the febrile, yet dominating image and voice of the man—such continues to be the prejudicial power of the screen image!—in the authoritative role of a priest offering (again, the suggestiveness of that other frail, yet dominating image!) his valedictory benediction, his *Guten Abend,* to the oppressor's world—this, without prejudice to a silent prayer to the ancestors that they withhold their summons to him for many more years.

Something continued to jar, however, and not even that autumnal image urging the resolution of all things made it easy to assimilate, within that same address, his unshaken adhesion to a matrix of intellectual and cultural values that singled out that same corner of world civilization for the redemption of humanity. And this complication of special pleading within a universalist theme is essential in our understanding of the hostility, or ambivalence of at least one-half of the colonial intelligentsia to the gospel of Negritude. Let us remind ourselves yet again that part of the problem was the Messenger, and the baggage of its gospelling, a strange advocacy that not only compromised the autonomy that Negritude, by its very nature, should insist on and by which it should indeed define itself. Such special pleading, too, was frankly irreconcilable with the historical context that made Negritude, a movement of protest, rejection, and racial recovery, inevitable. Senghor was easily the most articulate, indeed the most lyrically elegant poet of the movement, even though the expression—Negritude—was coined by the Martiniquan Aimé Césaire. Césaire's seminal "Notes on a Return to My Native Land" did not profess such cloying love for cultures whose histories and political conduct were clearly antithetical to the beingness of the black race.

We are obliged therefore to qualify the more common explanations that we frequently encounter—in critics and anthologists of the Ellen Conroy Kennedy, Gerald Moore, or Lilyan Kesteloot persuasion, for instance, and of a number of Francophone critics—that the hostility of the Anglophone writers—the English-speaking colonials—toward Negritude was based on a difference in colonial literary education—in short, that all that the creative conflict revealed was a clashing choice of stylistic models. This is far too simplistic a reading of the division that became prominent especially just before the independence of most African colonial holdings and during the first flush of literary output that accompanied independence in the early sixties. This analysis proposes that the Anglophone writers were strictly weaned on the poetic tradition of Ezra Pound, T.S. Eliot, Gerald Manley Hopkins, etc., and were

totally ignorant of the black American literary tradition—Claude McKay, James Weldon Johnson,
etc.—whose poetry the Francophone Negri-
tudinists settled on as models, after their rejection
of French mainstream poetics. The facts were
true, but that was not the reason for the cleavage
that was apparent in the various allegiances to and
alliances against Negritude.

Negritude Across the Waters

And that brings us conveniently to the origin of
the Negritude movement itself—that is,
Negritude but not by name—which, not surprisingly, is to be found, not on the café sidewalks of
Paris where Aimé Césaire, Léopold Senghor, and
others launched the journal *L'Étudiant Noir*, but
in American Negro poetry, and especially in the
writers of the Harlem Renaissance—Langston
Hughes, Countee Cullen, Sterling Hayden,
Claude McKay, and Paul Vesey. When you read,
or better still, listen to a reading of James Weldon
Johnson's *God's Trombones*, you can be left in no
doubt from what source the principals of the
Negritude poets derived their leaping meters and
rhetorical bravura, often tinged with the pulpit's

declamatory techniques. In any case, several of the Negritude poets, especially from the West Indies, acknowledged this debt, and engaged in a robust, creative dialogue with their American forerunners.

"The wind rising from black America," declared Etienne Lero in the first and only edition of *Légitime Défense,* "will soon sweep the West Indies clean, we hope, of all the stunted fruits of its outdated culture," while his soul mate, René Menil, in his own contribution to the issue, rejoiced that "the poems of American negroes are moving the world." Way back in 1925, Emmanuel Flavia-Leopold (to be harshly castigated by Etienne Lero for his "antiquated prosody") had at least translated both Langston Hughes and Claude McKay. The latter's *Banjo* became a bible for the new black consciousness; a new image of the Negro moved to oust the dominant, and bitterly resented, conformist representative of the "civilized" Negro of the West Indies, a product of "assimilation."

We were in contact with these black Americans during the years 1929–34, through Mademoiselle Paulette Nardal,

126

who, with Dr. Sajous, a Haitian, had founded the *Revue du Monde Noir.* Mademoiselle Nardal kept a literary salon, where African Negroes, West Indians, and Negroes used to get together.*

The French *salon* tradition was sufficient to attract these black intellectual writers and artists from different corners of the world, but there was also a sociological reality, consistently missed, that accounts for the deep empathy, a sense of special brotherhood, that existed between the Francophone emigrés and the American, one that left the British subjects as outsiders. Both, in contrast to the British-ruled colonials, were citizens, albeit alienated, second-class citizens—of "European" nations. True, in the case of the African continent, there was a further demarcation: the statutory French citizenry, usually those born in the colonies' capital cities and adjoining provinces

---

* L.S. Senghor, letter of February 1968, cited in Kesteloot. For a more detailed account of the interaction, see also Vaillant's chapter 4, "The Milieu of Negritude" in *Black, French and African.*

127

and—the rest. The educated Francophones however moved sooner or later into the citizen status, a prized achievement, as did Senghor when it became necessary for his educational advancement. This was a totally different state of social identity from the colonial subjects of the British both in Africa and the West Indies. The former—whether American or Francophone—were trapped in their socio-political bind; the latter, though subjugated, had no crisis of alienated citizenship to contend with. A foreign (British) power remained a controlling force, an alien presence in their midst; not so—needless to say—in the United States or the French Caribbean. And like the Negro of America, the French colonial found that the system at once identified and laid claims on him as a citizen of France, yet handicapped and disadvantaged him within that same socio-political framework.

This shared sense of internal alienation made the subject of art—the expression of life—a passionate field for its practitioners. Some form of exorcism was required by the artists; its agency would be sought in all disciplines—from political ideology to anthropology. From the one (Marxism), some found an ideal of universal

humanism that enabled them to diffuse the par-
ticularization of race into the less determinist
structures of class—it offered freedom in a new
consciousness and proposed a combative tool for
emancipation—in companionship with a wider
constituency of the oppressed. From anthropology, others (including some of the former) sought
to discover their roots, the meaning and significance of forgotten mores and values that could
then be forged into a distinct identity to be held
against others—nation and culture—that had
been merely bestowed. From within that past the
artists quarried a new language, new symbols and
rhythms that in turn reinforced that sense of a
separate identity.

There were uncertainties, of course. Even
between the Francophone Africans and the
French colonials of the West Indies, there
remained differences of both form and grasp of
content—not surprisingly—since sometimes the
journey into the past remained incomplete, even
superficial. As always, content is never divorced
from form, and the content that was appropriated
as the material of a new poetry was unevenly
absorbed, even among the most resolute in their
"return to source." A move toward stylistic

liberation in the arts, however, even by itself, remains a reflection, a craving for, or restatement of identity, a rejection of social categorization, leading, in most instances, to a recovery of and a revindication of some past (not necessarily one's own), or origin—the Renaissance, the Enlightenment, the pre-Raphaelites, the Expressionists.... Negritude. Once we concede that, we understand also that artistic renaissance is never an isolated event wherever the practicing artists are linked by a sense of identification, be it of race, religion, sense of origin, or social ideology. Style, in such circumstances, becomes a critical statement of intent, even in its groping, inchoate stages, a manifesto and shared instrument of self-liberation.

The struggle of the European colonies on the African continent and the Caribbean for their independence was never divorced from a consciousness of the daily reality of the degradation of blacks on the American mainland, the humiliation of political disenfranchisement, a daily habitation with casual lynching and the more structured judicial lynching that called itself judicial process. For instance, the trials and execution of nine blacks for the alleged rape of a white woman in 1950 earned the outrage of West Africans, expressed not only in the editorials of the media such as *The Pilot* in Nigeria, but in furious Letters to the Editor. Those who are familiar with a remarkable genre of pamphlet literature, known as Onitsha Market Literature in Nigeria, will come across plays, poetry, and polemical tracts that portray a vivid familiarity with the notorious episodes of racial discrimination in the United States, literature of rough and ready, combative quality. They move beyond generalized empathy and demonstrate an identification with actual details of the black man's continuing race-generated ordeal in the United States. The same creative vigor was evident in playlets and articles on the Mau-Mau liberation struggle that was then just beginning in Kenya. Today, these pamphlets are collectors' items.

The result is all too predictable, if we attempted to assess in whose favor the scales of reciprocation may be said to tilt—that is, between black American writers' reflection of the political travails and assaulted cultures of their kin on the mother continent and the reverse response, the reflection of black America's liberation struggle in the works of the Negritude poets. That the black American did look toward Africa for redemptive values is without question, but it was largely to a

131

nostalgic past, the past of a glorious history—
Egypt, Timbuktoo, Songhai, Zimbabwe, etc., as
statements in the nature of: "Thus we were!" The
Negritude poets also looked to the past, yes, but
as armory in the heated course of validating their
present and contesting the European denigration
of that past. A careful reading even of Du Bois'
The Souls of Black Folk, which was so seminal to
black thinking, would reveal that Du Bois was not
fully conscious of the affective *presence* of African
reality. Later, of course, he came to embrace the
politics and the leadership of the emerging independent nations, moving physically to Ghana
where he now rests. But his intellectual perception remained largely historical. He wrote of
Egyptian glory, the pyramids and the sphinxes
from which the black American glimpsed a vanished nobility, but in the African *past continuous,*
especially the cultural, he seemed blissfully disin-
terested. Those virtues that were singled out for
celebration in the poetry of Negritude—the black
race as the people of intuition, rhythm, and ancestral strength, as leaven for the reconciliation in the
dough of humanity—none of this was *real* or
applicable to self and community for the majority
of Negro American writers—Langston Hughes
always exempted. The mystic evocation of

Negritude poetry was, in short, missing from much of this American writing, Ralph Ellison notwithstanding. Samuel W. Allen was even more direct. In his essay, "Negritude and its Relevance to the American Negro Writer," delivered in Rome in 1959, he declared:

> I think there is little disagreement that our cultural situation is substantially different from that of Amos Tutuola, of Efua Morgue (later Efua Sutherland) of Ghana, of the Senegalese, resident of Paris since his university days, or of the Haitian or Jamaican writer. Our contact from Africa has beeen remote for centuries, and both the natural and the consciously directed impacts of the enslavement were to shatter the African cultural heritage. Further, the American Negro, uprooted from his homeland, has been subjected in a manner unparalleled among other peoples of African descent to the cultural imprint of a powerful, dominant majority in a strange and unfriendly land. The Ashanti, the Senegalese, the Yoruba were overwhelmed militarily and politically and

133

subjected to a foreign culture; but they were on their home ground, and retained the morale afforded by the mystic attachment to the soil of their ancestors.*

This wry lament is more than echoed in Claude McKay's *Banjo*. His character, Ray, was always conscious of a "missing link," an obscured source, which he recognized in his encounters with Africans from the continent. Awareness of its existence, however, strengthened him in his own confrontations with society, reinforced his self-awareness and confidence, integrating him within a larger family. It was a recognition that liberated him, buttressed by the knowledge that "he was not merely an unfortunate accident of birth."

Senghor's Muse of Forgiveness

Dominating the entire corpus of Negritude literature, however, was, inevitably, the direction of the subject itself—where should it head? And the

* See *The American Negro Writer and his Roots* (American Society of African Culture, N.Y., 1960).

divisions were not along the boundaries of language, but of vision and both creative and intellectual temperament. The dialectician in Jean-
Paul Sartre hailed its birth in virtually the same
breath as he elegantly wove its shrouds. He had
an unwitting ally in Senghor, for what can we
claim is truly left of the autonomy of Negritude,
of the repleteness of its conceptual being, if
indeed, as Senghor proclaimed, its destiny was to
be leaven for the exhausted dough of European
humanity? (Senghor also believed that the greatest world civilizations were the products of *métis-
sage*.) This view—regarding the destiny of
Negritude—was one that underwent various
degrees of refinement in an outpouring of poetry,
essays, and near-obsessive private conversations,
but retained its core creed. Indeed, as Senghor
grew older and memory impaired, it became a
common and rather sad experience for his associates, young or old, to encounter him at an event,
or at his home, and immediately find themselves
drawn into the same discourse in Paris or Stock-
holm at the very point at which it
terminated five, ten, sometimes fifteen years
before in Dakar or Tunis. Nothing more clearly
illustrated the obsessive hold on Senghor of an

idea that, I often suspect, was simultaneously hatched in his mind with the very emergence of Negritude—if indeed it was not Negritude's precursor. That central *credo* also suggests itself as a minor tributary to the larger stream of Senghor's Muse of forgiveness, for how can there be forgiveness, a harmonization of antithetical values, of action and reaction, of cause and effect, without a prior accommodation of even the negativities within such dualist tributary theses? That discourse, unsettling in the precision with which Senghor would resume it with you from a ten-year suspension, as if it had been interrupted only yesterday, is summed up in his contribution to the Second Congress of Black Writers and Artists in Rome:

> The problem we blacks of 1959 now face is to discover how we are going to to integrate African negro values into the world of 1959. It is not a question of resuscitating the past, of living in an African Negro museum; it is a question of animating the world, *here and now*, with the values of our past. This, after all, is what the Negro Americans have begun to do.

On the surface of it, unexceptionable. We are obliged, however, to recall those within the same movement who regarded such an agenda as suspect, indeed, a repudiation of memory and a call to race-suicide. It also obscures the view of the Muse of Equity, or Recompense, whose voices were never silenced in the dominion of Negritude. We shall listen to some of those voices, pausing only to insert the view that Senghor's stature within the movement is persistently attested to by the very passionate *critique* that his Negritudinist disposition still arouses among later generations of writers and artists. It is evident in the fruits of cultural transformation that he established in his native land, Senegal, the long roster of African poets who acknowledge their inspiration directly from the fount of his Muse even while remaining critical of his propositions, not forgetting the unique Festival of Black Arts of Dakar, 1966, in which he sought to concretize, utilizing all the media—music, drama, poetry, paintings, sculpture, and film—all that had merely been expressed in theory and in his own poetry. This festival, which united, on African soil, the children of the black Diaspora together with their living relations and ancestors, manifested the spirit of Negritude in a palpable way that had

137

remained unrealizable until then, providing, on the admission of the participants, a festal communion that has yet to be repeated in its selective judgment and intensity.

Lest, so soon after *The Open Sore of a Continent*, I be accused of an obsessive vendetta against my own homeland, upon whose shoulders the burden fell to organize the next black Festival of the Arts, I shall only observe that—yes— another black Arts Festival was staged in Nigeria in 1977, and that any participant in both should be addressed for a comparative assessment of the two events. One was adventure, revelation, a spiritual and artistic liberation; the other was vulgarity, philistinism, and—trauma! (Wild horses will not drag from me the secret of which was which!) Yet even that festival of 1966 was an opportunity not to be missed by our compulsive proselytizer; Senghor ensured that it also illustrated his unyielding theme of the *necessity* of cultural symbiosis, coopting all media of the arts, but especially dance, sculpture, and the revival of African tapestry arts—now given a Fauvist fervor—that he had promoted in Senegal. Senghor, as we have already stated, is nothing if not a consistent theorist, as well as a consistent animator.

No successful attempt can be made to gloss over the dilemma posed by Senghor, poet of peace and conciliator, so let us summarize it thus: articulating or celebrating memory, yet attempting to remain beyond its present impositions, is a feat that is possible only for a poet and priest, a contradiction that finds resolution in that elusive virtue that defines Senghor's "quality of mercy." It is of a different temper from that of Martin Luther King, whose quality of mercy is arbitrated with the rigor, not the catholicity of "love." Perverse though it seemed at the time—and is still thus regarded, to many of his critics and admirers—it is Senghor's, however, that now finds a prophetic resonance in the politics of post-Apartheid South Africa—a case of the poet yet again vindicating his role as one of the "unacknowledged legislators of the world"?

There is a tension in Senghor that is easily missed, thanks to his more intrusive plea for the remission of enemy sins, a tension that, like an internal dialectic within his poetry, leads to humanistic synthesis—and this is quite beside Jean-Paul Sartre's own dialectical structure of "anti-racist racism." Negritude came to mean more for Senghor than race vindication; it was to serve as a bridge into other cultures and racial propositions—*Arabicité, melanité, francité, luso-phonité*, etc.—as well as a tool for the retrieval of dispersed black races anywhere in the world—from India to Australasia. This was not a charge of the anthropological brigade to the rescue of lost black civilizations. Senghor's authentification of Negro presence in India—even to the extent of exploring the corpuscular proportions from blood samples and comparing cranial measurements!—for instance, became one proof of the "leavening destiny" of the black race in the humanization of the world. The syncretic achievement of black religions with Roman Catholicism in Brazil inserted "soul" as in religion into the "soul" of Negritude, vindicating for him, the direction of "oneness" into which his latter Negritudism evolved, and one that made his sermon of forgiveness, of reconciliation, both aesthetically seductive and humanistically enlarging. There, it does appear, our poet and preacher of peace does share common grounds with the *ordained* priest, Martin Luther King, who, however, in contrast, does not permit history to dissipate into the background.

But I find that I have no new tribute to pay

to Senghor beyond what I have written prior to his anniversary, and so I shall end with a passage from an essay that I wrote over fifteen years ago. It was published first in my collection of essays, *Art, Dialogue and Outrage*, under the chapter, "The External Encounter." It is one of those passages or statements that returns to haunt one for no just cause, inducing a kind of embarrassed squirming, given a turn of events that I certainly could not have foreseen at the time. It is of course an irrational reaction, but not even my notorious "A tiger does not proclaim his tigeritude" causes me half as much chagrin today as the following passage from that old essay. In the essay, I proposed that Senghor was "a true griot with a false vocation"—no, that is not the cause of the unease but what was to follow. In any case, I did proceed to extol the Senghor that truly trilled my poetic sensibilities like the strings of one of his own favorite instruments, the kora:

> (Senghor) is a nature poet, an open-air sensibility in whose veins the seasons of black Africa run their course with animistic ease; every breeze trills his tongue in epical tones, the heroic tonalities of

the born griot. He paints with bold strokes, delineating the shades and highlights of experience, spraying the patina of the eternal, of the secured communal (and ancient) reality. His incantations stretch the transient moments and emotions to rouse the ancients in their homes, joining the spiritual to the sensuous:

Young girls with upright breasts, sing the rise
of the sap proclaim the Spring

A drop of water has not fallen for months,
not a tender word, not a budding smile
only the fierceness of the harmattan, like the
    fangs of a viper
At best only a swell of the sand, only the
whirlwind of dust and straws and rubbish and
wingsheaths

Dead things under the fierce erosion of
* reason*
Only the East Wind in our throats like
* the cisterns*
of the desert
Dry. But this clamour in our limbs, this
* rousing of the sap*
swelling the buds at the groin of young
* men*
waking the pearl-oyster beneath the
* mangroves*
Maidens, listen to the song of the sap
* rising*
to your upright throats

And I concluded that section with these discom-
fiting words, which, I now reveal, were provoked
by the tiresome speculations and unseemly advocacies of some self-styled critics, a notorious sect
aptly dubbed neo-Tarzanists who had become
obsessed, even monomaniacal, with the business
of asserting who was deserving or unworthy of
what literary prize:

This is the Senghor we prefer to remember, the one to whom we wish someone would award the Nobel Prize for literature, so that the rest of us African writers can rest in peace for the next twenty years.

At first, I thought I had simply proved myself a poor prophet or had overrated my powers of *ase,* the ancestral voice of invocation. However, since winning that prize myself, and thus becoming inducted into the secrets of that shadowy Academy where these decisions are taken, I have been gratified to learn that those remarks very nearly proved prophetic, and not very long after I made them. The drama of that very near miss, however, is not one that I am permitted to narrate here—those secretive members of the Academy might decide to strike me off the roll for betraying their inner workings! Suffice it to say that, for me, Senghor remains the first—albeit unannounced—African winner of the Nobel Prize for Literature.

III

Negritude and the Gods of Equity

The continent of Africa in itself has remained a contentious object of contemplation and reference for black Americans and West Indians since the nineteen-twenties. "What is Africa to me?" was a question that inspired more than mere poetry and rhetoric—it informed, in one way or another, the socio-political existence of many. The paradox in several opposing attitudes—when we look at the polemics that ushered in the age of Negritude from the late twenties, in France especially—is that, without awareness of the fact, the rebels against the assimilationist tendency—Réne Meril, Etienne Lero, Léon Damas, etc.—were actually within the same camp as those identified objects of their contempt, the champions of assimilation such as the poet Gilbert-Gratiant, whose "This is my climate....the atmosphere of France" reads like an unconscious parody of Mark Anthony's "This is my space." This ironic link was that neither side, coming from totally incompatible ideological preferences, actually recognized in themselves subjects caught within the colonial vice. The French *assimiles* adopted the identity of France without qualification, indeed with pride and protectiveness; the "rejectionists," to whom the former were simply despicable lackeys and would-be black Frenchmen, were equally content to remain within the *French national* identity, never questioning its validity or potent contradiction to their mission of race retrieval. This blind spot in the latter group is easily explained. They were trapped within the raging ideology of the day, Marxism, a universalism that united the oppressed everywhere, without reference to color, race, or nationality. Thus, unlike their African compatriots, they did not stop to question their objective status as colonial appendages. *Decolonization* was simply not on the agenda of Francophone Caribbean, certainly not on the same level of intense awareness as we find among the colonial holdings of the French in Africa, and must be ranked even lower in comparison with the Anglophone. Although they also pressed the banner of artistic liberation—surrealism—into service as a counter to the stultifying bourgeoisification of the established, or up-and-coming African elite, it proved, because of its origination and allegiances, only slightly less than a willing surrender of the opportunities of a novel (or retrieved) identity in opposition to the established identity of others—which, in this case, was—like the artistic banner—European. Communism, surrealism, and Freud the European medicine-man—a perfect cocktail for nationalist amnesia! The reference points, and co-opted sources of the rejectionists did diverge drastically—they were certainly pioneering, more defiant and self-authenticating—from those of the genteel upholders of the *status quo,* yet both groups took their authority from the world ordering of yet again—the other. And there, of course, all common ground between these two camps—assimilationists and rejectionists—must be seen to terminate.

That there was an objective, historical, and therefore intellectual acceptance by the "radical

Africans" in the Diaspora of a necessary recourse
to Africa is beyond question. Even so, we recognize that among the French African nationals and
those of the Caribbean—if we may treat them for
now as one group apart from the black American
writers—there were also crucial degrees of difference in their respective creative "Negritu-
dinization." Politically, such differences virtually
did not exist. Across the board within Africa, that
is, throughout the literary and nationalist circles
of colonial Africa, the situation of the black man,
and the struggle of black leaders such as Marcus
Garvey—and indeed, of other charismatic champions who came later, such as the Rev. Adam
Clayton Powell—occupied the same territory of
political consciousness as the tribulations of a
Jomo Kenyatta or the calvary of Patrice
Lumumba. Mississippi, Alabama, Harlem—these
were household names, on the continent, that
narrated the black man's odyssey. Within the
creative-intellectual class, however, especially
among the poets, there were differences. The
Francophone writer-intellectual did absorb and
respond to these racial assaults through the
creative milieu to a greater degree than did the
Anglophone. The latter appeared to find a more

148

congenial medium of protest and rejection in nationalist politics—and the reason is to be found in the already stated contrast between the colonial policies of the French (or Portuguese) and the English. The impact of this difference is reflected in the relative emphasis given by these two principal groups of victims to art and culture as instruments of politics and liberation, long before Amilcar Cabral adapted the marxian discourse on culture to the liberation strategies of Guinee-Bissau.

The French employed a system of governance by what they called *départments*—the colonies, in other words, were treated as overseas departments of France itself. The colonial subjects were considered—or, more accurately, governed—as French citizens. Many of these figures were educated in France—from childhood, that is, unlike the British colonials who usually went to the United Kingdom only at the level of higher institutions. Even where the French colonial obtained his secondary—that is, high school—education in his own country, the curriculum was such that the school could very easily have been situated in metropolitan France. *My ancestors, the Gauls*...even some of the more conservative

Francophone poets felt humiliated to be compelled to intone such passages of educational initiation, meant for a different race and place; it featured constantly in rejectionist tirades and parodies. The British, by contrast, had no intention of insinuating such ideas of a shared ancestry into the minds of their subjects.

Intellectual interaction between French Caribbean subjects and the African—Senegal, Ivory Coast, Gabon, Congo Brazaville, etc.—was consequently much more fluid and constant than between Anglophonia and Africa, that is, between Jamaica, Trinidad, or Barbados in the Caribbean, and Nigeria, Ghana, Kenya, etc. on the continent. It is true that the British did import a handful of administrators, judges, and educationists from the Caribbean into their African possessions—today's shared existence of such family names as the Moores, the Thompsons, Cokers, etc. had its origins in this selective expatriation. For the French, however, it was regular policy. The black French Caribbean not only administered colonies, some headed military forces of subjugation for recalcitrant kingdoms. Others were noted artists, teachers, and scientific researchers. René Maran of

Martinique, the famous, or—from other points of view—infamous author of *Batouala,* was a notable product of this system, so were Paul Niger from Guadeloupe and Felix Eboue of French Guiana. The latter even earned the distinction of being buried at the Pantheon—for his political service to the French motherland *in Africa.* That posthumous distinction was only a kind of canonization of a living reality—a reality that placed the confluence of creative and political tributaries from French Caribbean and French Africa, carefully nurtured by the colonial midwife, in Paris. The British were far more bashful in encouraging fraternization on this level, fearful perhaps that the subversive germs from one part of the world might infect the other and thus create unwanted problems for the imperial mandate.

Next, let us recall the frequent incursions of the United States into the Caribbean. In 1915, and later 1927, the United States invaded Haiti—an intervention that would be replayed, albeit under different circumstances, seventy years later. There were also the U.S. recurrent interventions in Cuba, with extended periods of occupation—cultural compact with the Caribbean therefore rode on the back of militarist adventure; the United States proved an unwitting disseminator of the spores of nationalism and—Negritude! The invasion of Haiti had deep political and philosophical consequences, for instance, for the young poet and novelist Jacques Roumain who studied both in Paris and New York. His works came to the notice of Langston Hughes and Mercer Cook, who returned the compliment of Flavia-Leopold's and Senghor's translations of black American writers with their own translations of the Francophone. Jacques Roumain, already resentful of this violation of his natal space, a resentment that was augmented by his identification with the injustice under which his racial kin labored within the United States, would become increasingly radical and turn toward communism as a salvationist creed. That formative response of Jacques Roumain was not unique.

We can see therefore the route by which both French and Spanish Caribbean came to French Africa—via Paris—and why the wind of the Harlem Renaissance was felt so strongly in the café sidewalks and student attics where Africa's future Francophone poets huddled together to debate *la condition humaine*. Then there was the

Marcus Garvey phenomenon also, a movement that straddled both the United States and the Caribbean—Franco- Hispano- and Anglophone alike. The work of Jean Price Mars, the Haitian doctor, anthropologist, and passionate Africanist—*Ainsi Parla l'Oncle* (Thus Spake Uncle)— exerted great influence on Jacques Roumain, René Depestre, and their circle of radical nationalists, which was in turn transferred to Africa via Paris. "Thus Spake Uncle" remains a visceral call to a reconstitution of the authentic African psyche, and spoke to the French Caribbean—let us insert this footnote again—in a way that Du Bois' *The Souls of Black Folk* * could never emulate. Du Bois' work was directed more at the sociological condition of the black man in America, unlike Jean Price Mars', which targeted the psychological nerve. This restitutive anthropological manifesto was the element that was missing in the American response to Negritude. Yes, Langston Hughes and others did translate the Caribbean authors, published them in *The Crisis* of Harlem Renaissance, and even came under some influence

* *Three Negro Classics,* ed. John Hope Franklin (Avon Books, 1992).

153

of their thinking, but the American black writers had already mapped their course, had issued their manifestoes long before Etienne Lero's *Légitime Défense*. Claude McKay's *Banjo* was circulating among the young Francophone literati and Senghor would later translate Langston Hughes, Countee Cullen, and Jean Toomer—never mind that he found American poetry "non-sophisticated," or that Césaire would find in it "rhythms of juvenile spontaneity"—these were proposed as virtues, the very virtues they sought to free their own work from the restrictive molds of their French exemplars. Nothing of the dimension of this literary cross-pollination ever took place between the Anglophone Caribbean and black America on the one hand, and Anglophone Africa on the other. (There was, of course, no Alioune Diop in the British Isles, no inspired vision that could lead to the founding of a British *Présence Africaine!*) What we observe indeed is a paradox, that despite the United States being an English-speaking country, her black writers moved to develop a deeper creative and intellectual intimacy—via French Caribbean and Paris—with French Africa than they did with the British.

Cultural Assimilation—
The Politics of the "Refuseniks"

Language, therefore, it does appear, is not every-
thing, and we may bear this in mind in attempting to place emphasis on the peculiar circumstances that made the Francophone writer
respond to the colonial experience through literary tools and an artistic movement, unlike his
Anglophone counterpart. It was not simply that
Negritude appeared, in the main, to have created
a philosophical divide between the two; what is
interesting is that "Negritude," or indeed any
school or creative manifesto, was born in one, but
not the other. This is where we may find clues to
the differentiation. Cultural resistance manifested
itself in the Anglophone territories in more overt
ways, and almost always on the actual soil of the
colonies. There were certainly more newspapers
and journalists per square foot in Lagos,
Freetown, and Accra than you would hope to find
in a square mile of Dakar, Abidjan, or Gabon, and
nearly every one of them bristled with challenges
to the anomalies and injustice of their *colonial*
present.

Negritude—by any other name: It was in colonial Nigeria that the cultural liberation movement "Boycott the Boycottables" was launched by that nationalist firebrand, Mazi Mbonu Ojike—one could claim that Mbonu Ojike's movement served the same purpose in Nigeria as Damas' "inflammatory" lines from *Pigments* that led to the rejection of military draft in Ivory Coast. Ojike's gospel—which may have owed its inspiration to Ghandi's war against the British textile industry—was that Africans had become too dependent on European tastes, commodities, and culture. Anything that came from that other world was to be discarded—wherever possible—in favor of the local equivalent—clothing, shoes, food, ornaments, music, and—language. Ojike even proposed the abandonment of the English language and a return to indigenous languages for all internal communication.

Even the anti-colonial literature that emerged from this phase was not seriously considered as innovative or inspiring. These writers were considered forerunners to the tepid—though fiercely nationalistic—poetry of a group that came to be known within (Nigerian) Anglophonia as the "Pilot" poets—versifiers such

156

as Dennis Osadebey or—a name that should be familiar to all students of colonial politics— Nnamdi Azikiwe. They were called Pilot poets because they represented the early wave of published poets—from Nigeria at least—and their verses were published in a pioneer journal that started out in Ghana, moved to Nigeria, and was then known as *The West African Pilot*. Wisely, such poets decided that their real metier lay in direct politics, and Azikiwe, also known as "Zik of Africa," went on to immortalize his nationalism in the rhetorics of identity phrased in the language of "African irridentism" and "political risorgimento." He formed a political party, became a regional prime minister, and, later, served as the first Governor-General of an independent Nigeria.

Negritude. The African Personality. Authenticité. Boycott the Boycottables. African irridentism. Africanité. Back to Africa. Church of Ethiopia...etc., etc., etc. Even allowing for the opportunism that is embedded in some of these and allied rallying cries for a new socio-cultural order—and I believe that we can all agree to dismiss out of hand the Mobutu fabrication of *authenticité*, or the Eyedema mimic *Africanité*—

157

allowing for the purely rhetorical and diversionary ploys of any summons to an identity recovery, every one of such manifestoes directly implicates culture, and traces the trajectory of such culture backward into historic antecedents. This, really, is how the questions begin, how the "givens," the supervening arches of contemporary cultural constructs may be invalidated as lacking any authority in precedence, antiquity, and even—universality. Within Anglophone Africa, there was no shortage of these prospecting excursions into the subsidence of the past.

Within the Anglian outstation however, the Paris equivalent, black London failed to produce the equivalent of *Légitime Défense* or *L'Étudiant Noir*, although, of course, there was no shortage of nationalist pamphlets on colonial issues—or indeed on the rise of European fascism. Nigerian students were among volunteers for the International Brigade—one of them was a prince from my own hometown, Abeokuta. Researchers have found the Whitehall archives a fruitful hunting ground for numerous letters of protest, denunciations, and proposals on British colonial policies, covering almost every subject—education, trade, the Second World War, etc. The invasion of Ethiopia—then Abyssinia—was another important catalyst in the upsurge of cultural nationalism among the Anglophones, but we shall hardly encounter any literary reflection of this in the poetry of the period, even though it fueled the cultural discourse of intellectuals such as Edward Blyden or Casely Hayford. The inauguration of the pan-African conferences in Manchester did throw the British West Indians together with their African counterparts for the first time in any structured interraction, but the resultant manifestoes and plan of action were—political. No literary movement was born as a result of this seminal reunion of a people that had been thrust apart for centuries. Paris was a study in contrast, but, as we have outlined, this says as much for the temper of these two cities as it did for the colonial subjects who invaded them.

Paris was, after all, the intellectuals' and artists' melting pot of the world—to what other city did even the Russian emigrés flee, both under the Tsar and then, later, after the triumph of the Bolsheviks, to get away from the "dictatorship of the proletariat"? And the black Americans found the cosmopolitan flavor of Paris extremely congenial—for similar and different reasons—Richard

Wright, Mercer Cook, James Baldwin, Samuel Allen, or—from the world of theatre and entertainment—Josephine Baker and a trickle of jazz musicians that would later swell into a veritable stream. They did not choose Britain, which one would have expected to be preferable, from the language point of view. There was, of course, less *overt* racism in Paris, less obvious attitudes of discrimination. And I proposed, in my last lecture, the little-considered factor of a sense of affinity, of fellow-feeling between two sets of *citizens* at a second (internal) remove. Citizens, but not quite—one through the unfinished business of slavery, the other through an act of administrative legerdemain that conferred citizenship but recognized only subjects. Whatever the explanation, it was to Paris that they flocked. A notable exception was perhaps Paul Robeson. Yet even he, despite frequent visits to England, in concert and in theatrical performances on the British stage—in memorable roles such as Othello and Emperor Jones—even Paul Robeson did not really become part of the British artistic life. He was a familiar figure at the West African Students' Union, interracted with some of the most notable scions of Yorubaland who conferred on him the traditional title—*Babasale* of Lagos—but he had no influence whatever on a black artistic and intellectual community—because one did not exist. And Paul Robeson was also a frequent visitor to Paris, to sing at the *fêtes* of the Internationale and parley with officials of the Communist Party, of which he had become a member.

Those university and polytechnic students in England had only one ambition—to obtain their degree and return home. Home was not the United Kingdom. That was the essential difference between Paris and London, between the political and cultural policies of both colonial powers toward their subjects. For many of the intellectual elite of the French colonial empire, home was indeed Paris. The colonial departments of France elected black representatives into the French Assembly—Senghor and Aimé Césaire, Bernard Dadie of the Ivory Coast, Léon Damas from French Guiana, Rabemananjara of Madagascar, and a host of others were elected to the French Assembly. It would be impossible to find an ancestor of Wole Soyinka elected into the British House of Commons during this same period! The British Parliament kept its subjects at a distance. The reflection of black Diaspora in intellectual awareness therefore tended to be, for the Anglophone, largely political—a concern with the end of colonialism and the advent of national independence. The British colonial was not, like the French intellectual rebels, concerned with liberation from another culture, for the simple reason that, in the main, he had no experience of a cultural *loss* or alienation. It was this mood that you will find reflected in the journals of the period and the genre of mostly agitprop literature that I have already referred to, including poetry of a rather middling literary quality in some of the aforesaid journals.

The French intellectual was—as a result of these policies—a deracinated individual. French colonial intent was to turn its captive intellectuals into Frenchmen and women, to assimilate them into French metropolitan culture—and, for nearly one long century, it worked! The rebellion against this policy, one that found it difficult to express itself in political action—the French were ruthless colonizers!—commenced after the military conquests cited by Samuel Allen, and found its outlet in the much safer battleground of culture, fueled by its contact with American writers and intellectuals, and the immediacy of the more

162

cruel and overt racial negation experienced by their kinfolk in the United States. This was quite a potent mixture, one that would affect even the more accommodating Senghor. For others, it aroused the battle cry of identity in a far more direct language that would occasion grief for some of the practitioners, including spells in French prison for racial incitement. So, the battleground of culture was not really as safe as we may have appeared to present it. The "love" of Senghor's expression for the French nation was an ambiguous relationship whose obverse stung several of his contemporaries—stomping the same cultural and intellectual battleground—into increasingly aggressive positions.

Etienne Lero, the uncompromising one, articulated this relationship most fiercely in the one-time manifesto of his group, *Légitime Défense*: it rejected the French Parnassian tradition of poetry and exhorted its readers to seek their models of inspiration from Surrealism—and from the literature of the American Negro Renaissance. *Légitime Défense,* even more than *L'Étudiant Noir* of Aimé Césaire and Senghor, was so confrontational in its denunciation of French assimilationist policy, so politically leftist in orientation—it endorsed communism as the path of liberation for the black race and all humanity—that it was banned by the French government after its very first issue. Jacques Roumain, Etienne Lero, René Depestre are not so well known as Senghor, Damas, and Aimé Césaire but, without question, this trio—and also some of the better known names—represented the non-negotiable sector of the province of Negritude.

In Léon Damas, for instance, we encounter even the undisguisedly anti-French dimension of Negritude in an exhortation to Senegalese soldiers *not* to rush to the defense of France or consider her war with Germany any of Africa's business. "Invade Senegal," cried Damas, and he meant invade and conquer colonial Senegal, recover the authentic Senegal from her colonial domination—not merely of nation but of culture:

> *To the Senegalese veterans of war*
> *to future Senegalese soldiers*
> *to all the Senegalese veterans or soldiers*
> *that Senegal ever will produce,*
> *to all the future veterans*
> *former and future regulars*
> *what-do-I-care future former....*

Me / I say SHIT / and that's not half of
it

Me / I ask them to / shove / their
bayonets / their sadistic fits / the feeling
/ the knowing / they have / filthy / dirty
/ jobs to do

Me / I ask them / to conceal the need
they feel / to pillage / rape / and steal
to soil the old banks of the Rhine anew....

Me / I call on them / to leave the Krauts
in peace.

This, need one comment, is a far cry from
Senghor's benediction on the Seine—that placid
symbol of French cultural inspiration, of its bour-
geois-artistic, as well as its radical artistic soul.
Léon Damas' poem was considered treason.
Unlike Senghor, Damas does not call on any
christian god to assist him in reining in his serpent
of hate for the white race—he unleashes it in full
venomous lunges:

My hatred grows
around the edges of their villainy

the edges of the gunshots
the edges of the pitching
of the slave ships
and the fetid cargo of the cruel slaves

White

My hatred swells
around the edges of their culture
the edges of their theories
the edges of the tales
they thought they ought
to stuff me with.

Oppose Damas' response to their "theories" and their "culture" to Senghor's prayer for the redemption of "France, who expresses the right way so well." Damas is not prepared to grant even that intellectual concession to France. In yet another poem, "So Often," he declaims:

And nothing
nothing would so calm my hate
as a great
pool
of blood
made

by those long sharp knives
that strip the hills of cane
for rum

Unfortunately, this is not the kind of writing from
the contribution of Léon Damas to Negritude literature that finds its way into the mainstream
anthologies. The more transparent, obvious, and
rather sentimental verses of his black assertion
tend to find more ready space:

Give my black dolls back to me
So that I can play with them
the simple games of my instincts
instincts that endure
in the darkness of their laws
with my courage recovered
and my audacity
I become myself once more
myself again
out of what I used to be
once upon a time / once
without complexity....

Ay, there's the rub, there is the major bone that
stuck in the throats of the anti-Negritude writers.
"Give my black dolls back to me," I wish to play,

"the simple games of my instincts," "what I used to be / once / without complexity." In such lines, we encounter the disquieting other side of Léon Damas, seemingly—that is, when taken out of context. There we find him out of tune with radical militants such as Réne Depestre, Aimé Césaire, etc. There he appears to have fallen into the trap of the Negritudinist summons to something worse than a paradisial idyll—a state of infantile regression, no less. Unless one sees the poetic output of Damas as a whole, unless one situates such occasional slips into jejune romanticism within his rejectionist, non-assimilationist, and rounded political intelligence, one reads immediately only the tract of Negritude at its most superficial and undialectical.

Foul! cried the opposition in response to such versification. This was playing the European game of racial condescension. In their ears rang the Albert Schweitzer doctrine: the black man is my brother, but a junior one. The black man is simpleminded like a child. A creature of instincts, not of rationality. Any complex processes of phenomena elude him. Aimé Césaire, even within the context of his brilliant epical indictment of history, his celebration of the black man's combative destiny, has been propagated largely through those passages that appeared to be an endorsement of the David Humes, the Gobineaux, and other philosophical racists:

Aeia for those who never invented anything
Who never explored anything
Who never conquered anything

This, many pointed out—and quite rightly—was a travesty of the black man's history. Without calling it by name, Kwame Nkrumah opposed such a doctorine with the political and historic construct of the "African Personality," set up ideological schools that traced the origin of mathemathics to the black man and credited none but the black race with the construction of the pyramids. So did scholars like Cheikh Anta Diop who was not merely a Francophone, but also a Senegalese, that African end of the axis of Negritude. So it was not just a Francophonie versus Anglophonie affair. But what claims precisely did the Negritudinist proselytizers establish, in order to balance this seeming negation of the black man's contribution to world culture? Aimé Césaire was certainly not proposing a void to counter the overproductivity of the European. Neither was Senghor. What they proposed, quite simply, was a revaluation of neglected humanistic properties. A mystic wisdom that defied materialism and, of course, in Senghor's case, a priestly benediction—an infinite capacity for reconciliation.

Dolls of Innocence or Masks of Assertion?

The clock—a mechanistic invention, and a linear apprehension of time—was to be discarded, smashed. Let the European inventorial mind be controlled by time; the black race was the fount of timelessness and thus the guardian of the very immensity of creation. What is not subject to regulation or measure is infinite, and this was appropriated as the province of the black race's essential being. Bernard Dadie, for instance:

> *I have carried the world since the dawn*
> *of time*
> *and in the night my laughter at the*
> *world*
> *creates the day*

His black hands, Bernard Dadie proclaims, may be calloused from the injustice of history, but

even deeper than Aimé Césaire's fingeprints on
the skyscrapers of New York:

*I plunge them / into the earth / into the
sky / into the light of Day / into the
Diamonds of night
I plunge them into the morning dew /
into the gentle Twilight
into Past Present Future*

Or Birago Diop's justly famous *Soufflés,* sometimes published in English as "Breath," or
"Spirits"—or as "Ancestors"—in Langston
Hughes' translation—but one that may justly be
considered the poetic exegesis of animism within
the movement, that unique spirituality of the
African that establishes a continuum between the
worlds of the living, of the ancestor and
the unborn. The animist grace is made to imbue
the Negritudinist sensibility with an essence that
was safe from appropriation by the European or
the christian, yet contested the combined hierar-
chies of their materialist orientation on the one
hand, and their spiritual ordering of the world on
the other. This essence is rooted in the rituals and
observances of African societies even till today, lies
at the heart of their artistic intuitions, and

establishes a solvent for pantheistic resolution of all spiritual urgings:

> *Listen to Things / More often than*
> *Beings / Hear the voice of fire /*
> *Hear the voice of water / Listen in the*
> *wind / To the sigh of the bush /*
> *This is the ancestors breathing*
> *Those who are dead are not ever gone*
> *They are in the darkness that grows*
> *lighter*
> *And in the darkness that grows darker*
> *The dead are not down in the earth*
> *They are in the trembling of the trees*
> *In the groaning of the woods*
> *In the water that runs*
> *In the water that sleeps*
> *They are in the hut, they are in the crowd*
> *The dead are not dead.*

This mysticism bears no relation whatever, and owes nothing to the European Surrealist venture that formed yet another paradoxical tributary to the Negritude movement—we shall touch on the nature of that paradox in a moment. Birago Diop's mystical exploration of the African world-view was a total derivation from source and from source alone—he was, it should be noted, a veterinarian who spent a lot of time among his people, in the neglected rural areas. Birago was no frustrated creature of French alienation. This background distinguished his poetry from, for instance, that of Rabiarivello, the tragic Madagascan poet, who was a product of the movement, but not truly a part of it. Rabiarivello occupied a very special creative space, unique to himself, and untouched by many of the social concerns that relieved other poets from the danger of alienation and a total retreat into a solipsistic creative existence. We point to Rabiarivello—and Surrealism—only as a productive instance of the many tributaries that flowed into, and the branches that sprouted from, a movement that was not quite as homogenous as many critics sometimes present it as being. Rabiarivello's true mentors and models were Verlaine, Rimbaud, and Baudelaire, with whom he shared, in the words of Ulli Beier, "a disgust of reality." This response to reality was, of course, of a different order from the animism of a Birago Diop, who sought to penetrate beneath reality to extract an other-reality that is interwoven with the physical, and opens itself to a pantheistic universalism. Senghor attempted to distinguish it from surrealism by naming it surreality, while I once manufactured "animysticism" as my contribution to this quest to trap the ineffable in the concreture of words— I doubt if any "naming ceremony" will ever prove lasting, or satisfying.

If Rabiarivello's poetic bent led him to a self-absorption off which social challenges bounced easily, with social indifference, the same was hardly true of his neighbor islander, Edouard Maunick, of Mauritius, whose self-definition—in contrast to the majority of the Negritude poets— took a rather cavalier, yet tortured attitude to the past:

> *I no longer need the past / To stand up*
> *in the present.*

Now, reminding ourselves that Edouard Maunick was part Indian, part French, and part African— a common enough mongrelism on the little island of Mauritius—almost in equal parts, we see indeed that Negritude posed a subjective problem for quite a number of its adherents. Maunick solved this very simply by declaring: *J'ai choisi d'être nègre* (I choose to be black)—in his poem of the title "Seven Sides and Seven Syllables" from *Carousels of the Sea*, applying, in effect, the arbitration of the sword to the external imposition of a Gordian knot, and proposing a direct solution to a questionable dilemma of choice. That question appears settled, but Maunick does return to it in various forms, and with occasional ambivalence or, more accurately, qualifications:

> *If I could find a kingdom*
> *Between midday and midnight*
> *I would go forth and proclaim*
> *My mixed blood to the core*

And, still from the same poem "Seven Sides and Seven Syllables"

> *I the child of all races*
> *soul of India, Europe,*
> *my identity branded*
> *in the cry of Mozambique*

The summation remains the same, however, and Maunick proceeds to identify with—as indicated in that last line—and react to the political plight or adventure of the community of race. When you share identity with "the wretched of the earth," other identities take second place or appear comparatively academic. Maunick belongs to the second generation of Negritude poets, by the way, after Senghor, Damas, Césaire, etc. His visit to Yorubaland (in Nigeria) in the early sixties—his first ever—merely intensified a choice that he then extended to cover the entire racial experience wherever it was to be encountered. Personal humiliation was identified with distant assaults— like the lynching of Emmet Till—the young boy whose alleged crime was that he smirked or whistled at a white prostitute. This was a traumatizing incident of race aggression that moved him to bitter lines, as it did an impressive number of poets within the movement. Its tragedy and timing posed a racial challenge, providing an immediacy that yanked both the first generation Negritude poets and their successors from their more abstract preoccupations—Aimé Césaire, David Diop, Léon Damas, and all. Or Tchikaya U'Tamsi from the Congo, whose own route to reconciliation and forgiveness we have already remarked, and is reflected in the elegiac tone, an intensely controlled anger, of his own lines to Emmet Till:

> *I am no longer master of my time*
> *Master of these greynesses of time*
> *What flowers can I weave for Emmet Till*

176

the child whose soul in mine
lies bleeding ....

I die alone from pride
I leave to Emmet Till his death
from horror at myself

Even more lacerating is the rage of an Aimé Césaire, of Birago Diop, or, most belligerent of all the Negritude responses to such assaults, the poetry of René Depestre. Using the voodoo gods of his Haitian island as a structure of revenge, Depestre's *Epiphanies of the Voodoo Gods* makes a visitation to an imaginary Alabama family and avenges the humiliation of the black race. It should be noted that *Epiphanies* is, to widen its thrust unambiguously, actually a section of the collection, *A Rainbow for the Christian West—* with its paradoxical symbolism that merges with yet cancels the accommodativeness of a Senghor—"no more floods, the fire next time."

One by one the gods emerge, and no prince of peace any of these, but agents of retribution... Atiibon Legba from the Guinea, Ogun Ferraille and Shango from the Yoruba, Damballah-Wedo from Dahomey, Agassou, and that original creation of the islands themselves, Baron Samedi. The concourse is for a time of reckoning, not of understanding or reconciliation. The warsome face of Negritude is unleashed by René Depestre, unrelieved by any tender lyricism:

> *I am Agaou native of Guinea*
> *My lizard when he bites white flesh*
> *Does not let go until the*
> *Thunder of the revolution growls*
> *I know the art of binding up*
> *Your rains, your prejudice, your fantasies*
>
> *I am Baron-la-Croix*
> *The dog that howls at death*
> *In your garden is me*
> *The black moth*
> *That flies about the table is me*
> *One word too many and I'll transform*
> *Your little southern lives*
> *Into as many crosses*
> *Forged in the iron of my soul*

There is no comparable work on that theme from Anglophone Africa—to find equivalents of response, you must research the journals, and the proletariat pamphlets whose contents were not truly considered as inspired or inspirational literature. But let us also include a little of the prose-poem sections of the same work to provide the full inquisitional temper of this outpouring of an embittered soul, one that coopts mythology directly into the services of a revolutionary reversal against the oppressor. It is taken from the section, "The Bath at Dawn."

> *Now, dear Alabama family, drop your last illusions at my feet! I am going to dissolve all the white dirt that human folly has accumulated even in your hearts. I am a god in sixteen persons and tens of other minor loas pulse on the same wave length as my blood. I make the tour of your house mounted on a magnetic goat. Look at the eyes of my phosphorescent mount. They ask you the following two questions: What have we done, we, the wretched black men of the earth, for these Whites to hate us so? What have we done, Brother Depestre, to weigh so little on their scale.*

Thus, in direct terms we encounter the same question that was being asked—in various degrees of passion—by the liberation movement within

the United States, a question that was either presented in rhetorical fashion, or one whose answer
was deflected into artistic channels; for even if no
answer was ever really expected, if the answer
remained unfathomable to the oppressed black
mind—and why should it not remain so, since,
until the white encounter, such a mind had no
concept of itself beyond a daily apprehended
human repletion, creative and intellectual certi-
tude of its existence and valoration—it remained
a puzzle that had to be exorcised. It was no accident that a near identical phrasing appeared in
that same *Letter from Birmingham City Jail*:

> when you suddenly find your tongue
> twisted and your speech stammering....
> when you have to concoct an answer for
> a five-year son asking in agonising
> pathos: Daddy, why do white people
> treat colored people so mean?

For both priest and poet, for both poet of
vengeance and priest of remission, this was an
underlying question and recognition that
launched the quest for Negritude. "The Negro
past," "Egypt, of the black Pharaohs," "Black
consciousness," "Black is Beautiful," "the African

Personality," etc.—and Negritude the creative sanctuary—they are all responses that lament of a René Depestre and others, in varying degrees of anguish and bewilderment: "What have we done, we, the wretched black men of the earth, for these whites to hate us so? What have we done...to weigh so little on their scale?" It then moved beyond the rhetorical stage and sought answers. It was phrased as a liturgy of racial exorcism and, for the victims of French colonial alienation, Negritude provided the vessel of the exorcist creed, extolling the recovery of identity. And even those who, like Edouard Maunick, claimed:

I no longer need the past
To stand up in the present

nonetheless do go on to declare:

Identity is proof of the grandeur of man,

while Aimé Césaire sweeps up all the negative imagery that had ever been bestowed on his race and declares: Yes, if you do persist in such negative attribution, let that indeed be the identity. But now it is I who will it. I refurbish it all in the light of recognition, of acceptance. I refurbish it and transform it through the magic of the creative intellect. I bless the labor, the degradation. I baptize it all Negritude and I define it within the totality of my image. The world that has been produced, after all, by the self-proclaimed superior world, does not exist, could not have existed without that denigrated presence, so let us celebrate it even as once given by—the other!

> *And I tell myself Bordeaux and Nantes*
> *and Liverpool and New York and San*
> *Francisco*
> *there is no place on this earth without my*
> *fingerprinting,*
> *and my heel upon the skeleton of skyscrap-*
> *ers*
> *Who can boast of more than I?*
>
> *I accept....I accept....I accept...entirely*
> *without reserve*
> *My race that no ablution of hyssop and*
> *lilies could purify*
> *My race corroded with stains,*
> *Ripe grape for drunken feet*
> *Queen of sputum and leprosies*
> *Of whippings and scrofula....*

I accept, yes, says Césaire, your impositions and your definition. The distillation of it all has gone, however, into an insurgent weapon of self-recognition, affirmation, and proud annunciation:

Those who invented neither gunpowder
nor compass
Those who never knew how to conquer
steam or electricity
those who explored neither seas nor sky
But those without whom the earth would
not be earth....

Or to revert to the earlier particularisms, those without whom San Francisco would not be. Not San Francisco not Liverpool, nor Paris. My fingerprints are everywhere, declares the poet, my creative sweat is mixed up in its mortar. And within such a summative understanding, much can be forgiven even of negative hyperbole, otherwise known as poetic licence. "Reason is Greek, emotion African" is one of the most notorious of such hypberbolic manichaisms, but if we penetrate into the heart of the poetry of what can be interpreted as racial slander, if we expand, just for the sake of argument, Jean-Paul Sartre's dialectical situating of Negritude as anti-racist racism, we begin to appreciate such hyperboles as metaphorical weapons forged in the heat of contestation.

Let us put it this way: it is as if you persist in

calling me an idiot. For a long time, I protest, then, one day, I discover a way of silencing you. I startle you by responding, one unexpected day, with the joyous shout: yes, of course I am an idiot, but, for a start, have you read Dostoyevsky's *The Idiot*? Now, that would be more than sufficient for a non-African black who has only attained the confidence of Negritude via the filter of European humanities. Imagine, however, if he was also a Yoruba, or has acquired sufficient weaponry from the armory of Yoruba humanities! Again, twisting the blade of denigration from the hand of the racist, he would demand, "And what do you know of the deity Obatala, the god and protector of albino, the cripple, and other disadvantaged of humanity? What do you know of that mysterious confidant of the gods, the 'touched by the gods' whose interior language of communication you interpret as idiocy?" The "idiot" did not await the birth of "political correctness," the coy acknowledgment of the impaired of society under cosmetic names in order to be admitted into the world of the "norm," or the privileged. His being *was* from the beginning, and society recognized him as one of the children of the gods, and not even of a "lesser" one. Césaire's embrace of the negativism of others, which he then addressed as a "positive" of his race's *a priori*, was ultimately unanswerable—"his (the black's) treasure lies in those depths disdained by others."

The wounds of that "disdain," however valiantly its depths are appropriated and willed into its own antithesis through the transfiguring power of poetry, remain part of the scars of African history. It is futile to pretend that the scars are not real, or that contemporary actualities, like the effects of a change of weather on certain dormant, or muted ailments, do not re-open such wounds. While "the children of a lesser god," secure within their world ordering, may dismiss the other's contraction or belittlement of their universe, the fact remains that the other has impinged on it in a way that permanently precludes the solace of remaining within the secure isolation of its own precedent world order, or whatever vestiges of it are left. In short, the effects of that "disdain" appear permanent, inescapable; they are to be read in a thousand and one actualities that plague the continent, and can be measured in the retardation of social existence against the visible prosperity of the other on a shared planet. Memory, however fitfully obscured, retains a record of that inequity—inequity because the prosperity of one is not unrelated to the circumstances of the spiritual and material impoverishment of the other. This is no newly discovered wisdom. Let us remind ourselves of the existence of a vast array of works that exist on this theme through the appropriate choice of two (non-black) scholars who, three-quarters of a century ago, reinforced the convictions of these pioneers of race-retrieval that crystallized in Negritude—Delafosse and, yet again, Georges Hardy. The former wrote (in 1922), of the pre-islamic African state, as it existed in 1353, that is, before the commencement of the Arab slave raids and later, European, and colonization:

> a real state, whose organisation and civilisation could compare favourably with that of Moslem kingdoms and of the same period

while Georges Hardy (1927) bluntly declares:

> Islam began the work of destruction...but Europe did a better job...not only by separating and destroying the races, but by systematically disorganising....

186

It is always useful to recall that the acknowledgment of a history of "disdain" has not been
limited to the memory of its victims alone, nor to
the passion of their poets and griots, scholars and
ideologues.

A Lesson from the Balafon

Let us take ourselves back to that pre-enslavement
season of a continent, to that pre-islamic period of
African statehood from which Delafosse selected
his example. During that century—indeed, for
some time before—and for centuries that would
follow, quite a few empires would rise and fall—
Ghana, Mali, Songhai, etc. Mali is the center of
our interest for now then known as the
Mandingo empire. It is the year 1230, or there-
abouts, and a war is fought between Soundiata
Keita and Soumare Kante, the king of Soso. In
the famous battle of Kirina, King Soso is defeated
by Soundiata. You will find the details of that battle in the epic of Soundiata. That narrative, like
the legend of Chaka the Zulu, remains to African
literature what the Viking sagas are to
Scandinavian countries, the Arthurian legends to

the European, or the *Odyssey* or the *Iliad* is to contemporary world literature.

It is not, however, the battle or the literary classic itself, or the feats of empire-building that constitutes our point of reference, but a little musical instrument called the Sosso-Bala. This instrument had been made by Soumare Kante himself toward the end of the twelfth century. Legend has it that its fabrication was inspired by genies, and is endowed with a supernatural, even sacred character. Soumare Kante became so enamored of this creation of his that he reserved to himself the right to play it, exclusively.

After the battle of Kirina, however, this instrument, the balafon, fell to Emperor Soundiata as a war trophy. He placed it in the custody of his personal griot, Bala Fasseke Kouyate. For eight centuries, the family of Bala Fasseke has remained guardian of the sacred instrument, which, however, remains the property of the descendants of Soundiata Keita. It is the symbol of the Mandingo empire, which once covered today's republic of Guinea and neighboring territories. That instrument remains today under the personal charge of the Republic of Guinea.

Now what has the Sosso-Bala got to do with

poetry, Negritude or anti-Negritude, with the Muse of remission, or the deities of rigorous equity? A lot, actually. Quite a lot. The immediate connection is that I first set my eyes on this famous instrument in, of all places, Paris. This was the instrument's first ever outing since it fell to Emperor Soundiata—the guardians have never permitted it to leave its place of habitation since it came into their custody. An exception was made on this occasion, however, for none other than Léopold Sédar Senghor, whose ninetieth birthday we had all gathered to celebrate. The balafon, like the kora, not only has inspired much of Senghor's poetry, but is constantly celebrated in his works. Both the balafon and the kora—but the kora especially—are instruments that often accompany the griot—the original poet, epic narrator, and custodian of history of the peoples of this part of the world. The poetry of Senghor is propelled— as has been perceptively remarked by analysts of his works—by the pulsating energy of the tradi- tional griot, a leaping rhythm of self-surmounting ocean waves that is brought to the service of a variety of themes and subjects, even non-African ones. It was only fitting that this rare presence— the Sosso-Bala—should provide the climax, the *pièce de résistance* of the three-day celebration.

Fortunately, the ancestors were in favor—
they were naturally consulted through divination
rituals. It was one thing for UNESCO, which
keeps record of tens of thousands of such patri-
monies—from the monumental to the miniatur-
ized—it was one thing for UNESCO to take the
initiative, and for the government of the Republic
of Guinea to give its assent, or indeed the insur-
ance companies to agree to insure such a priceless
object for heaven knows how much—all that came
to nothing if the rituals were not made, and positive auguries obtained from its divine protectors.

Well, what was the crowning moment like?
We had waited in great anticipation. The Sosso-
Bala was in fact a day late—the ancestors
obviously operate a different time schema from
airlines but, finally, a group of five musicians
appeared on stage. A long piece of cloth was laid
on the ground and then—in came *the* balafon,
swathed in nothing more than what looked like a
casual dust sheet or a woman's light wrapper. It
was carried under the armpit just like any other
instrument of its kind—the balafon is quite light-
weight as you know—just a xylophone. Pieces of
wood laid over an array of irregular sized gourds—

the resonance chambers—and beaten by two sticks with rounded heads. The wood appeared unpolished, revealed no suggestion of pedigree timber, the strikers were neither ebony nor ivory.

Yet there, right before us, lay eight centuries of history, poetry, of pride, inspiration, and sacred heritage. A simple, unassuming xylophone that was, however, born out of conflict, of a bloody struggle for power and the travails of nation-building, yet innocuous in its appearance, at once an embodiment of history, yet insulated from it, giving off its own statement of harmony and resolution that constitutes both its reality and innate contradiction. That balafon was redolent with ancestry, a survivor of much bloodshed and human loss, before and beyond the incursion of aliens east or west, of even yet unresolved conflicts, a statement of the complementary truths of strife and harmony—indeed, to revert to my own symbolic world of deities—a testament again of Ogun, the god of war and destruction, of the lyric and creative spark, a protagonist into unsuspected realms of existence and consciousness—including the world of moralities.

It struck me, on first reflection, as a perfect metaphor for literature itself—and especially for

191

literature that is the product of crisis—both the crisis of some origination that is external to the literature itself and that—the more common—of crisis within the creative being. But then, I was in the process of preparing a lecture titled "Literature in Crisis," and this was a haunting metaphor that was clearly in search of an anchor and was quickly grabbed by the first viable comer. Today, I am inclined to expand that metaphor beyond literature, and the claims of the present cooption are certainly even more firmly grounded; it is merely returning the metaphor to its source or, as Senghor might prefer to phrase it, to a "Negritude of the sources"—in this case, the Muse of Reconciliation, of which Senghor is himself the lyric acolyte.

And the sound? Well, again, an anti-climax. It was no Stradivarius of xylophones. A crisp, aged tonality, but nothing extraordinary, no mystic resonance such as the flute of Orpheus was reputed to have had, or the magic pipes of Akara-ogun in that Yoruba classic, *The Forest of a Thousand Daemons*. A few tentative notes, welling into a confident seam, then the voice of the female griot joined in, filling the auditorium with the plenum of history from which that instrument, the choir on stage, and we the black listeners had emerged, but the resultant harmony was one that enfolded the gathering in a mantle of humanity that excluded none, neither the colonizers nor the colonized, neither the slavers nor the enslaved, the disdainers or the disdained. That moment was the obverse face of the earlier narrated sensations of the Ouidah slave route, yet it settled into a near identical residuum of that earlier experience. It was a dirge of ancestral severance, of loss too great to quantify, only benumbing, yet filled with evocation of a quiescent triumph that is an extract of human resilience, of a shedding of individuation into a tide of universal affirmation of a humane oneness.

Perhaps it is within this territory that lodges the impulse of forgiveness, since oneness eschews distinctions and makes war and peace, creativity and destruction, guilt and innocence, Negritude and tigritude, Senghor and Depestre...all facets of an irreducible humanity and thus steers that dichotomized, even fragmented entity toward a resolution within an anterior harmony. I do not really know, and I possess neither wish nor temperament to abandon the continuing, combative imperatives of the dialectics of human history. But such glimpses and echoes of the possibilities of harmonization do surface periodically as consolation, and can open up horizons for a humanized vision. Within such a context, the Sosso-Bala becomes an unsolicited metaphor for the near intolerable burden of memory, a Muse for the poetry of identity and that elusive "leaven" in the dough of humanity—forgiveness, the remission of wrongs, and a recovery of lost innocence.

Index

195